THANK YOU FOR WALKING AWAY

THANK YOU for WALKING AWAY

HOW TO OVERCOME LIFE'S CHALLENGES AND DISCOVER YOUR PURPOSE

ANGELINA ROSARIO

www.mascotbooks.com

Thank You for Walking Away

For more information, please contact:
Mascot Books
620 Herndon Parkway, Suite 320
Herndon, VA 20170
info@mascotbooks.com

Library of Congress Control Number: 2020910270

CPSIA Code: PRV0920A
ISBN-13: 978-1-64543-306-4

Printed in the United States

This book is dedicated to my nieces, Ricely, London, and A'niyah, who made this book possible. You guys are my "why" behind this book. I knew if I finally started living my inner truth, I would be able to share the wisdom and blueprint I learned along the journey. I want you to understand what is "true power and self-love." I hope after reading this book, you will always own your truth. Your story is your power—period. Don't ever dim your light or compromise your happiness for any relationship. The same strength in me is also in each one of you. Life will have many ups and downs, but look at everything as an opportunity to grow. Don't ever compare yourself with anyone else. God gave each one of you a specific gift. You were created to be great! Now, go out there and live your best life.

INTRODUCTION

Heartbreaks are hard, but what's even harder is if you do not realize that the moment he walked away was also God's way of letting you know you were about to get off at the wrong exit, and He had to redirect you. The best thing that ever occurred to me happened the moment when my four-year relationship ended. The journey had its high moments and troubling ones, but they were all intended to guide me to this very place I am in life right now—talking to you, letting you know the best thing he ever did was eliminate himself out of my life. Smile, girlfriend, you are meant to shine, and I am going to show you how.

This book manifested because I used the pain of heartbreak to push me towards my true calling. I hope this book does the same for you. Life does not just happen; it happens to propel you closer to your true self. Allow life's encounters to be the very things God uses to fulfill your dreams. This book is going to tell you how I decided to seek God after my breakup, but then ended up in other dysfunctional relationships, and shortly after was diagnosed with a tumor. Yes, I went through two terrible seasons in my life at the same time. I was causing some of the hurt I was experiencing by not listening to God's instructions.

This material will help you realize your actual value and the high plan God has in store for you. Mark 9:23 states, "All things are possible if you believe."

You can have it all right now: God, health, love, joy, family, and a career. It is really up to us as women to make a conscious effort not to ever settle for anything less than the best. To understand that life does not just happen, but it unfolds through how we decide to live it. Even when nothing seems to be happening, everything is happening. I once heard, "The teacher is always quiet during a test." God is always working on our behalves, even when it does not appear to be so.

People always come up to me to tell me how beautiful I am, and based on my career and job title they assume I have it all together. However, the reality is there was a time when I did not. Many nights I would come home lonely, asking God why He still had me in a desolate place. I didn't see it then, but I see it now—this time in my life was preparing me for the best version of myself. I wanted a quick fix. I didn't want to deal with my demons. I wanted God to fix everything as soon as possible. Even when it came to writing this book! God told me a year and a half ago to start, but I kept pushing it off. I said, "God, what in the world—write a book? For what? What's so different about me? Why do other women need to hear my story?" Again, I procrastinated for as long as I could. It crossed my mind at least two to three times a week, but I did not want to confront it. I did not deem myself worthy enough to be able to touch other women's lives.

I pray that after reading a few chapters of this book, you will re-evaluate your life to see what areas you need to improve. Trust me; I have done a lot of improving in my lifespan. I worked for corporate America and left to become an actress in Los Angeles, opened up my non-profit organization, dated successful men, and came back to corporate America. I have achieved a lot and made many mistakes, but I have also learned a lot in my journey. I want this book to give you hope and a reason to achieve your goals in life, no matter what life throws at you.

CHAPTER ONE

HOW IT ALL BEGAN

Before we get into why you need to thank your ex for walking away, I have to take you back to where it all started. I'm going to share my story so you can understand nothing happens by chance. You will also come to know that you are not alone—we all go through some hurt and pain.

Back in April 2012, I was a sales executive for a radio station. I wanted to do more, so I started a makeup line. I planned to resign from my current company in November 2013 and pursue my career in the entertainment business as an actress, have my makeup line, and be a wife and mother. I had it all planned out . . . or, at least, that was what I thought. At this point in my life, I became an "expert" in creating my goals and excluding God from them. I never took the time to ask God if this was His plan or not.

I was thrown a curve ball in the midst of planning my resignation when my general manager at the time asked me what my future career goals with the company were—I was at the peak of my career, having had the top sales as an account executive for two consecutive years and achieving all of my sales goals. He felt I was ready to grow beyond my current role and move into management.

I didn't know how to break the news to him that I was planning to resign in a few months and venture into other endeavors. I also wasn't getting along with my direct manager and felt maybe it was a sign for me to part ways with the company. I was torn and didn't know what to do. I thought about it for a week and finally decided to put my name in the hat. My boyfriend at the time told me I should pass on the opportunity since we were planning on relocating to Los Angeles. He felt it was a waste of time to apply, and I was better off giving another person that opportunity.

What I could not understand was this tightness in my stomach and the whisper in my ear saying, "Apply for the position." I told myself it was going to be impossible to get it, since I had no prior management experience and over fifty people were applying for it. However, I could not ignore the knot in my stomach and the small whisper, so I applied for the job.

Weeks went by, and I did not hear anything about the other candidates or if I was being seriously considered for the role. In fact, I started to understand more of God's voice, but at the time did not know it was God giving me instructions. At that time, I was much more religious than spiritual and when things like this would happen, I would not pay much attention.

It came down to two candidates: another person in the same department I worked in and me. I do remember one morning as I was praying I heard a small voice say, "Tell the other candidate that if she gets the job, I will follow her lead." Startled, I opened my right eye and told myself, "WHAT THE HELL?" Yep, exactly what I said when I heard it during my prayer. I said to myself, "I am legit crazy—this cannot possibly be of God. God knows I am a naturally competitive person; He can't possibly be asking me to follow these absurd instructions."

That same day, I was walking down the hallway heading to the bathroom. She walked by, and I could sense my spirit telling me to go up to her. God set up the scene for me perfectly, and I was still too hard-headed to follow through with what the whisper had asked me to do. It was like God was checking to see if I would obey. I, of course, failed and failed miserably, because not only did I ignore God's instructions, I straight-up pretended not to see her.

The following day as I was praying, I heard the same voice again. I told God, "Lord, come on, is this you? I am starting to feel crazy." The next day the candidate walked by me, and I knew I had to relinquish my ego and tell her what I heard the Lord tell me. I passed the test this time around—I was surprised at how she received what I said. After I disclosed to her what God had told me to say, she proceeded to hug me. God used that small conversation in the hallway that afternoon to start a spiritual friendship for a season, a journey neither of us were expecting to embark upon.

It was hard for me to understand what God was doing. My personality was not one to allow people into my life quickly, especially someone I felt didn't have my best interests at heart. Thank goodness for God's word. Isaiah 55:9 says, "As the heavens are higher than the earth, so are my ways higher than your ways and my thoughts than your thoughts." God's ways are opposite of ours. The whole matter was confusing to me—I did not know as much as I know now about being obedient to God's guidance, but I knew I needed to pass the test. Don't get it twisted, it took everything in me to pass the test, but I can tell you it was worth every bit of difficulty.

What I can vow is that God's instructions and directions will make you feel like you are demented. You cannot lean on your own understanding, but understand there's a significant reason why He is asking you to do certain things in a specific manner. Don't try to alter His plan to make it work for you; follow wherever He leads. There are times I will not tell my friends or family about significant decisions because I know they are not going to make any sense to them. If God gives you precise guidance or directions, follow them. He will not ask us to do something unless it is going to bless our lives—He knows what is best.

Don't look back at your life and feel like you missed out on a career opportunity or got into a relationship you should have avoided because you were too bullheaded to do what God asked you to do.

I cannot begin to fathom what would have happened if I ignored God's instructions again that afternoon in the hallway. Yes, I failed the first time, but God is such a graceful God. He will give us another shot. I learned a lot from that one situation; you have no idea in what form your blessing is coming. You have to be obedient to what your gut and the Holy Spirit are guiding you to do.

I was promoted to local sales manager shortly after. I feel sometimes God wants to see if we mean it when we say, "Lord, instruct my footsteps, and I will follow."

Thank God I obeyed and applied for the position. Soon after my promotion, my ex and I separated. I didn't see this one coming—out of nowhere, with no signs at all, my boyfriend at the time decided he didn't want to be in the relationship anymore. Can you imagine if I would have ignored the voice? But again, let's thank the one who broke our hearts. God allowed it to happen because He knew He had a bigger plan for me.

When he walked away on July 8, 2013, my spiritual journey started. I never thought I would experience the most painful, fulfilling, and majestic journey. It has led me through a lot of ups and downs in the past five years, but most of all this journey has taken me to a place where I would learn most about myself: the flesh, insecurities, fears, and lack of self-worth that all resurfaced through the five-year journey after the breakup.

I remember the day like it was yesterday. My ex decided that he wasn't ready for marriage and that it was best to part ways. I remember feeling lost and conflicted. How could someone I loved so much out of nowhere decide this relationship wasn't for him and he had to go? I was left questioning God. The bizarre thing about it all was from the moment he told me that he couldn't move forward with marriage, he ultimately turned cold and became a person I had never known in our four-year relationship. It all goes back to the day I decided to take matters into my own hands and go ahead of God.

Back in May 2013, I gave my ex an ultimatum that if he didn't propose to me by September of that year, the relationship would be over. In hindsight, it probably was the most prominent learning lesson, but also the biggest blessing. Signs from the spiritual realm were making it even more apparent that this relationship was coming to an end. When we got home that night, he decided to tell me he wasn't ready for marriage and proceeded to tell me that while I had grown a love for God, he was still questioning God's omnipresence. I could see his soul had darkened.

If I can be honest with myself, God started giving me warnings months earlier about our relationship going downhill, but I wasn't present . . . or, maybe I just refused to pay attention. However hurtful it may have been, it also was the beginning of finding out who Christ was in me. My search for why I was even in this world began. All of the answers didn't come rushing to me right away, but I received the right amount of information and experiences every step of the way.

God had to put me on a path, and many times I took a detour because it was taking too long to get to what I wanted. I wanted instant gratification, and I wanted it NOW. I thought I could take matters into my own hands, but doing so only led me to more and more destructive relationships. I tried to speed up the healing process, thinking to myself, "I just need to be in another relationship, and I will get over my pain." I was trying to find a quick fix to suppress the hurt I was feeling. The only way to have proper healing was to do it with God. When I kept putting myself on a dead-end route, God made every attempt to protect me, but I chose to ignore him.

I wanted to control everything, even time and order, and that's not how God works. When you are running from yourself, you end up forgetting who has total control of your life: God. He does give us free will, which includes the choices we make. It's crucial to be present and clear-minded when making decisions, especially when it comes to dealing with relationships.

I did have all types of mixed emotions since I didn't understand why God would give me one thing and remove another. All I kept hearing was a soft voice saying, "Let go and let God." I kept hearing it over and over again. I know our plans don't always go as planned, but this was very unexpected and hurt so much. I was hearing a voice from God, but it still didn't take the pain away. I cried for many months, but there was strength in me that kept me going. I knew God must have had a greater plan and would somehow help me.

I lost ten pounds shortly after my breakup. I was in a new position—not everyone I worked with was happy about my promotion, including the sales managers—and the love of my life completely decided to walk away. I was so lost and confused. I didn't know what God was doing with me. I've always been a tough one in the family—the one who could handle it all without being vulnerable, and for the first time in my life, I felt helpless. I needed help and didn't know where to turn. I cried more than I slept. I had to put on an act in front of people, which took more energy than just being real. I wanted to run away from everyone. Have you noticed running away was always my go-to?

One afternoon I was about to close my office door because I needed to cry. I was hurting so bad and felt no one could understand the pain I was enduring. The candidate who was in the running for the promotion walked by and noticed something was wrong with me. You see how God works? He used the last person, someone who basically wouldn't say more than two words to me, to comfort me in one of my weakest moments. Her exact words were, "I felt like I was having an out of body experience. I didn't want to check on you, but my spirit was going towards you, and I had no control." When she walked into my office, she hugged me so tightly, and I just started crying uncontrollably. Who would've ever thought God would use her, out of all the people I knew, to be the person who gave me the strength to get back up at that moment? We both felt God's presence. And yes, that's how the Lord works.

Sometimes we are too blind and our ego kicks in. We will block our blessings because His way is not the way we would do it. In return, our friendship led her back to Christ. You see, we were both being used for God's purpose but didn't know it then. And even though we have gone our separate ways, I know she came into my life for a reason, and for that she will always have a special place in my heart.

God has taught me that He will bring different people into our lives for different purposes. I've also learned we all have our own journey, and as you are growing spiritually and trying to figure out the next step, you will have to leave people behind. Not to say they won't be in your life at all, but they are just not heading in the same direction God has for you at this time. I've learned how to detach myself when God tells me it's time to let go. I believe to reach your highest potential, you have to follow your own personal legend, which will have lots of ups and downs, and the miracles will come from the most mysterious places.

My life was changing very rapidly and I was being led on a spiritual journey, though I didn't understand it fully. I felt challenged in my new position, but since I was distracted by my personal life, I didn't put much thought into the drama at work.

I got through it every night by praying and asking God for strength. It didn't occur to me that I needed to figure out a plan to salvage the relationship. Trust me, I didn't understand it at all, but I knew I had to go through it. I didn't realize it would cause me to grow and push me to become who I was destined to be, but thank goodness I accepted God's plan and dealt with the pain. Don't try to fix what God allowed to fall apart. You will miss out on what you are supposed to be doing in the next chapter of your life. It will hurt and there will be moments when you don't even want to get out of your bed, but keep going. There is a reason things are happening the way they are. If you get out of your head, you will be able to move beyond the pain.

Prayer is powerful here. There's no way I could have gotten through with my sanity and integrity if it wasn't for the power of my Holy Savior Jesus Christ getting me through. My girlfriends always think I'm so strong and fearless, but that's not true. I do get weak and crazy thoughts running through my mind, just like you, but I don't depend on myself—I release it all to God and ask for the strength to cope during that season. He will start sending you people, resources, and tools you were never exposed to, to grow you and push you closer to your purpose. But the reality is, many women miss these gifts because they go after things that God never intended them to fix. They beg for the man to stay or degrade themselves to get the man's attention. If you have done this, it's okay—it's a new day. If you haven't, please don't fall into this path. A week after my breakup, a friend called to check up on me. I was so distraught, I sounded very resentful. Every word coming out of my mouth was completely out of my character, and in some sick way it was boosting my self-esteem. My friend had already started his spiritual journey and could hear my anger. He told me I was dealing with an ego problem and was going to send me a book that changed his life: *A New Earth: Awakening Your Life's Purpose* by Eckhart Tolle. Of course, I took it like any prideful person would, personally, and told him, "I don't have an ego problem, and keep the book." Well, he sent it anyway.

I remember receiving the book and saying out loud, "Why did he send me this book? This is so stupid, and I'm not egotistical!" I didn't understand the dynamic of the ego yet. I was in denial. I was a zombie, sleepwalking in this world. I was blaming everything on my ex instead of sensing the opportunity this breakup was about to give me. God was giving me small signs about what He was about to do in my life, but because I was so disconnected with the present moment, I didn't see them.

I came home from work the day after we separated and noticed that his belongings were all gone. While sitting on my ottoman, all these feelings of abandonment that my dad had awakened within me during my childhood came to the surface. I thought to myself, "Why am I even thinking about my dad?" What I didn't realize was that I never dealt with my daddy issues. You see, from a baby until eight years old, I was extremely close to him. I was raised in Miami in a very unfortunate neighborhood, made up mostly of single mothers living in the projects and on welfare.

My mom and dad never lived together and had a very strange and dysfunctional relationship. Many times, I witnessed my dad cheating and beating my mom. I would stand behind a wall to watch, hearing my mom hollering and crying. It was hard taking it all in at such a young age. As a result, my mom became abusive and took her hurt out on us, especially me, as I was the oldest in the household. She would beat me for no specific reason. I became an adult at a very young age. I had to take care of my two little sisters while my mom was working two jobs to keep a roof over our heads.

When I was eight, my dad decided to vanish and abandon my mother, leaving her raising three girls on her own in the ghetto. I would say all odds were against us, but now I understand that we can rewrite our stories, and just because this is how our story began, it doesn't end there.

I realized that I've never paid attention to the hurt and pain. I suppressed it over the past twenty-three years. I thought it didn't even matter that my father abandoned me. It wasn't until my ex walked out of my life that I realized this was more than just about him. There were things that I hadn't dealt with in my own spirit.

Now, don't get me wrong, it didn't change the fact that I was angry, hurt, and confused about our separation, but now I was dealing with the root of all my pain. I got upset with my dad and fell on my knees, not understanding why all these feelings were coming up or why a man would reject his kids. I knew I needed help, but didn't even know where to start, so I ignored the pain and went on for a few months, trying to ignore what I was feeling. I didn't want to look vulnerable, especially in front of people who thought so highly of me.

Two months later, my ex-boyfriend texted me. I missed him so much that I quickly picked up the phone to call him. I told him we needed to talk in person and he owed me an explanation; after all, we were together for four years, and I thought we would be getting married and building a family together. I was trying to control the situation.

I flew out to Brooklyn with every part of my being saying, "Don't go," but I went anyways and stayed with him for the entire weekend. I went to his basketball game and tried to rekindle what we once had, but I could see in his soul that he was struggling. The day I was leaving he said he couldn't move forward, and it was best if we just permanently parted ways. Ouch! Again, I put myself in a situation to be broken. I distinctly felt in my heart that I shouldn't have flown to New York.

He would randomly text me with, "Thinking about you, love you," and this, of course, would bring me to tears. A few months later, my ex reached out to tell me he would be playing against the Miami Heat and wanted to see me because he missed me.

We spent an entire week together, but on the last day in Miami, he told me he wasn't sure what he felt toward me and needed to let God guide him. I sat on my seat at the American Airlines Arena with this knot in my stomach, unsure how to receive the news. I do remember hearing a soft whisper in my ear and heart telling me, "Let go and let God." I wanted to tell him, "Please don't do this to us again!"

But something in me (the Holy Spirit) helped me refrain from saying such things. I complied with the soft voice within me. I walked away from the arena with tears in my eyes and with all this agonizing pain. I was questioning myself and wondering why this was all happening. We'd had such a wonderful week together. I even asked God, "Why would you bring him back just to remove him again?"

I had all these questions with no answers. All I heard was, "Let go and let God."

I Don't Have Exes, I Have Y's. Like "Y The Hell Did I Date You?"
The Rebound Guy #1 AND #2

I was tired of feeling the pain, so three months after last seeing my ex, I decided to respond back to someone who I used to date back in 2006. I figured it wouldn't hurt if I could at least have someone to entertain me. I cut him off the first time because he wasn't a man of his word and I had caught him lying a few times. I thought surely after seven years he must have changed and matured. He seemed to be closer to God and wanting the same thing I was seeking: marriage.

I started dating him a bit more seriously, and he flew down weekly to see me. I knew the moment I saw him that I shouldn't be dating him again because I was still in love with my ex. Again, I chose to ignore my inner voice and went with the flesh. Shortly after dating for a while, I realized he was still the same person I'd met in 2006. He hadn't changed. He always had the bad behavior of not being able to keep his word. I knew this seven years prior, but I chose to ignore what I already knew for instant gratification. I just wanted the pain to go away. Instead of taking the time to get to know myself, I decided to get into another relationship.

Of course, I wasn't in this relationship for long before I heard God's voice one night in Atlanta while having dinner with him. "He's not your husband." Now I was dealing with daddy issues, a breakup, and hearing the voice of God saying, "He's not your husband." I was back to square one and didn't know what to do, so I decided to end things with him.

I felt like my back was against a wall, and I knew God was the only one who could give me peace with my current situation. I started going back to church, feeling like I would surely find peace there. I wanted to learn how to be content wherever God had me. I immersed myself in God's word and learned as much as I could about God. I even started going to service on Wednesdays. I probably became an extremist, but I knew it was something I needed at the time.

I was starting to get to a place of peace. I wasn't crying as much, and I was learning a lot about who God created me to be. I still had issues I had to deal with, but the church did bring joy to my heart. I changed some of my lifestyle behaviors and started meeting new people and doing new things. It felt great changing my environment, even if it was just for the present moment.

God knew what He was doing with me, and I just had no idea where this whole journey was taking me or why it was all happening until I reverted to my old ways.

I met someone at church who was very attractive and intelligent. As you can see, I had a pattern of not wanting to be by myself. I justified my actions by saying, "Well, I met him in church—he could be the one." I remember vividly standing by him after a Sunday service, and I heard this voice come over me, saying, "This is not your husband." I thought I was hearing things. This can't be of God. HELLO, I'm in my church home. I even remember laughing to myself, saying, "I hear things. I think I might be going crazy."

I wasn't going crazy; it was God guiding me. But I must admit, I was one stubborn person. I used to debate even with God to prove my point, which of course only got me so far; nowhere, actually. Every time I was around this guy, something in my spirit kept telling me something was not right—and sure enough, it wasn't. I realized it soon after and cut ties with him.

Awakening Moment

I started listening to Eckhart Tolle—yes, the one I said I didn't have to read because I didn't have an ego. It's okay to laugh at my pain now. Timing in life is everything. I was starting to get a better understanding of God from a spiritual perspective and not from a religious one. I wanted to get a better understanding of who I was and what my purpose was in this world. I was hurting so bad and couldn't stand the fact that I had no control over anything in my life. I had to feel the pain and be in the moment.

At the time, I hated every bit of having to go through this. I didn't want to deal with myself and didn't think I was the problem. Surely it had to be all the guys I was meeting who had problems. I shook my head as I wrote my last sentence. You have to realize it's not them, it's something about you that keeps attracting these types of men. Trust me; it was hard to keep it one hundred with myself. But acknowledging the part we play in our own unhappiness is the only way we grow and stop repeating vicious cycles.

There are lessons in every situation you get into, and until you learn from these you will continue seeking the same thing, not knowing why you keep getting yourself hurt. I had to realize I was attracted to a specific "type" of man. I never consulted with God about whether this was what He wanted for me. I wanted what I wanted and that was it.

It wasn't until one day a few years later that I had some quiet time to reflect on where I'd been and where I was currently. I realized something so vital—I wasn't the person I wanted to attract in my life. I did love God, but there was still a piece of me who was very much caught up in the worldly ways. My own insecurities were bringing me the same type of men. Like attracts like, and unfortunately, I was seeking men to tell me how beautiful I was to just build my ego. It was all ego. The men were usually in influential positions, but those are often the ones who deal with so many insecurities.

Now, let's think about this: two insecure people equal a dysfunctional relationship. There's no way we can build a strong foundation when our base is built on ego and pride. None of these men were genuinely walking in God's light. They loved God, but there's a big difference between believing in God and walking with God. We would have conversations about God occasionally, but there was no depth. There was no way I was going to grow spiritually by continuously dating men who weren't genuinely walking on God's path. I had a lot of hard knocks, but thankfully, God never gave up on me.

If you are wondering why the situations you are getting yourself into are not working out, this could be one of the reasons. It's time to stop and have a real conversation with yourself. You have to be brutally honest with you. You also have to bring this conversation to God. He will somehow in His own mysterious but wonderful way start to provide you with people and resources to work on this.

What's cool about this whole process is that when you meet someone, there may be things about him that you know aren't exactly traits you would want in a husband—and let me make this clear, I'm not talking about the outer characteristics, but his heart and actions. You will pause to reflect on yourself to see precisely what it was that attracted this person to you, and you will ask God to reveal if you too have these types of traits. It does become quite fun, if you don't take yourself so seriously, and understand this is a new journey you've undertaken. The goal each day is to become a better version of yourself.

Romans 2:1 says, "You, therefore, have no excuse, you who pass judgment on someone else, for at whatever point you judge another, you are condemning yourself because you who pass judgment do the same things." How beautiful are God's words? He's telling you when you pass judgment on others, you are just passing judgment on yourself. Instead of giving an opinion on the person's behavior, figure out what is it about you that needs to change so you can stop attracting these types of men into your life.

I felt my love life was crumbling while everyone else's around me was flourishing. There was a time when I was the only one in a relationship, and now I was the single one and everyone around me was getting married.

My oldest sister was getting married to her boyfriend of six years in the Dominican Republic. I dreaded having to attend the wedding and be around people in relationships while I was still dealing with a broken heart. I was there with a fake smile, pretending that life was perfect, when deep inside I was hurting and just wanted to run away from everyone, including myself. Has this ever happened to you?

Oh, it gets even better. Shortly after my oldest sister's wedding, my middle sister was getting married, and to top it off she made me one of her maids of honors. I even told God, "Lord, you truly have jokes. Why do you have me a part of all these weddings when this is the very reason my ex and I fell apart?" I wanted to go somewhere far away, somewhere no one could find me. Everyone around me was getting married and having kids, while God still had me in the same place . . . or, at least, that's what I felt. I would later find out that this place was exactly where I needed to be. This was where seeds were being planted to help me become more of my true self.

I was so excited when all the weddings and pregnancies were all over. Yes, it sounds horrible saying this, but that's where I was in life. Have you ever found yourself in this space? It's a test to see if you will be happy for others, even when things don't seem to be going all that well for you. Pass the test! Be pleased when your family and friends are receiving the things you've been praying for, because it's a wink from God, who is showing you to wait on Him because He has a divine plan designed just for you. Timing in life is everything! You have to trust God will give you what you've been praying for in your due season. You don't want to force anything. Yes, you can push marriage and end up divorced five years later, or end up pregnant but single. God hasn't forgotten about you!

He has hand-selected the husband for you. You have to continue pushing through it all. The only thing that kept me going was the word of God. Trust me, you don't want what they have. I'm not implying what they have is inadequate—what I am saying is that you want what was explicitly sketched just for you. There is an individual plan. Impatience will create a frustrating and regretful life. You will find yourself miserable and unhappy in the long run. It's best to be single now for a few months or even years than go into something that will leave you broken-hearted.

Don't get caught up in what is happening in people's lives. I know it is easy to become bitter, or even resentful, when you feel like God has forgotten about you or forsaken you. He hasn't; it's just not your timing. You have to accept where you are in life and the decisions you've made that have led you there. Don't you go pointing fingers— we all have choices, and every opportunity comes with consequences. You are putting yourself in harm's way with every dinner date you say yes to, without first asking yourself, "Does this man have the qualities I'm looking for?" I know you are probably wondering, how would you even do this if you hadn't gone out with him yet? It's easy—by having a few conversations with him, you will know if he has at least a few of the building blocks you two will need to build a strong foundation. In later chapters, I discuss what you need to be doing in this season.

You just pick up your chin, Queen, because you were destined to live a life of greatness. God is not trying to withhold anything or anyone from you. But He does know us and how our immaturity can sabotage our blessings. You have to become a particular type of woman, which you can only do through God, to be able to sustain the marriage He will bless you with. I know you feel like you've been ready and God is punishing you. I want you to stop thinking these foolish and negative thoughts. You are a child of God! He wants to bless you, and not only for you, but for the world to see His miracles in your life. Why would He withhold anything from you if you are ready to receive? You're just not there yet, and it's okay. The great news is, when your time has arrived, it won't be a second early, nor a second late. Is it wonderful to know even though it may not feel like it at the present moment, everything is right on schedule? You should be jumping with joy when you hear this. John 13:7 says, "Jesus replied, 'You do not realize now what I am doing, but later you will understand.'" God knew we wouldn't understand His plans in the present moment, but He also said later on we would. Have complete confidence in God's plan, even if you feel like you don't know why life is unfolding the way it is.

Go to that wedding, dinner with your married friends with babies, engagement party, and baby shower with faith and confidence that God has already heard your prayer. Enjoy these types of events; it may be God giving you a glimpse of what He's planning on doing in your life.

It took me a while to understand it, so please learn from me, this is not God punishing you at all. You should be happy for your family and friends who are celebrating such things in their lives. This is not the time to start feeling like you are a loser and have missed the train.

This is the time for you to rejoice with a joyful heart. Your time is coming and will be much better than you ever expected.

Now, let me take you to when I was starting to awaken spiritually. I started learning more and more about being in the spirit versus being in the flesh. I was questioning things that I'd never wondered about before. I began looking at the world from a different set of eyes. Even with all the tears I had cried since the split, I knew something was happening in my soul. God was getting my attention for a reason. The awakening of our true self is fundamental to be able to step into our God-given purpose.

One afternoon, I had a moment of realization: I'd never been single. I'd jumped from one relationship to the next. I never gave myself enough time to heal, learn about myself, or reflect on what I learned about my previous relationship, so I took all the baggage and mess into the next relationship. I was seeking a love only God could give me. Of course, I didn't know this at the time, and I wasn't surrounding myself with people who knew this information, either. It was an ongoing pattern for years, and it was starting to feel as though I was having internal conflicts. I was fighting with my flesh and my spirit.

I couldn't understand why I was beginning to feel a conviction deep within my soul. I knew God wanted me to follow Him and trust Him, but I felt like I was being pulled into two different directions. I was also yearning for a man's love. I didn't know how to be by myself. I kept running into the wrong arms. I would ignore all the red flags, thinking it wasn't a big deal. But it was a big deal, it was going against who I was in my core. When you find yourself battling with a man's behavior, it's because your true essence knows what you deserve. Yes, there are times you will have to compromise, but the big rocks, you can't.

I kept ignoring the significant issues, the ones where I knew I was selling myself short. The relationship would end, leaving me distraught, but I never took the initiative to address it with myself, so it would spill over to my next relationship. I was trying to learn how to become better in this area, and every area, of my life.

After a year of attending the church I'd joined, I felt it was time to venture off to another church. I even dreamt about it, and I asked God to let me know what I should do. God does answer when you ask Him to give you clarity about a particular situation or direction. I ended up at Universe Truth Center, where I would learn about everything that I was already experiencing. The metaphysical space was happening right before my eyes, but I didn't know what it was.

Being raised in a religious household, I always looked at things from a black and white perspective, but God is so much bigger than that. There are just things no one but God has done or will do. No man on Earth can ever explain exactly how God does things. I got a better understanding that nothing happens by chance. God has ordained every step of my way. Proverbs 20:24 states, "The Lord directs a person's actions. How then can anyone understand their own way?" Here I thought I knew it all, but I didn't know how my life was about to unfold. I wasn't supposed to figure out my entire life, I just needed to take one step at a time.

After getting a more precise vision that God orchestrates everything in this universe, I understood there was a purpose to the pain I experienced from my ex walking away. The revelation into my new journey gave me peace in my heart, even though I was still grieving. I made up in my mind that I would set sail on my new adventure with a new attitude and not get stuck as a victim. I didn't want to make any excuses about why I couldn't get through this stronger and better than I was at the time. It was up to me to get my thoughts under control and move them into a positive space.

I started reading all sorts of empowering books. I wanted to learn from the greats who had gone through these types of heartbreaks but came out like winners on the other side. I was thirsty and hungry for growth. God never intended for us to get stuck on the battlefield. He wants to use our pain for good, if we allow it. We do have control of the way we look at sorrow seasons in our lives. The knowledge I was gaining taught me new ways of looking at the world and my circumstances; it was stretching me into thinking more like God and less about myself. My breakup or your breakup wasn't to set us back; in fact, it was to get us going in the right direction. So, please say, "Thank you for walking away" to the man or men who have walked away from you. It was all done for your good.

During this season, I started seeking like-minded people. God began to do things right before my eyes, but as I was beginning to embark on this new journey, another test was thrown at me, a test I failed to pass and which took me backward before I was able to move forward.

CHAPTER TWO

THIS SINGLE "THING" SUCKS

One night, I attended an event the company I work for sponsored. Honestly, I wasn't trying to be there, but was advised that all sales managers had to participate. Later in the evening when things were unwinding, my coworkers and I walked out, and this guy who worked with me approached me. I had seen him around, but had also heard rumors that he had been pursuing me for a couple of years. He told me that I looked gorgeous, which led to a quick conversation. He texted me later that night, and the conversation led to many more conversations, and then into a relationship.

This guy and I couldn't have been any more different. He smoked, drank alcohol like it was water, and partied like a rock star. I wasn't a goodie two-shoes, I had my issues, but his lifestyle was very different from mine. My downfall was I had a mouth on me, and if words could kill, I probably would've been killed a million times. I stayed with him out of fear, afraid that this was the best I could do, and I didn't want to be single.

Ladies, what a terrible place to be. Desolate emotions will make you do things that are so out of your character or belief system. God gave me several dreams about my partner being a party guy, even cheating on me, and I ignored them all. I was too afraid to face the truth. Every time I was with him, I could hear this soft voice saying, "Angelina, this is not your husband," but I was over the little voice. I didn't want to hear it anymore. Everyone around me was in a relationship and I felt people would think something was wrong with me if I was single.

I had this image I was trying to portray and was doing anything possible to make sure no one thought I was hurt. Even though deep in my heart I knew I shouldn't be dating him, I also didn't want to feel that lonely feeling. I was devoting my life to God, but still battling with the flesh. He literally would take everything I said and would turn it around and make me look like the bad guy. When a relationship is from God, you won't have an ongoing battle with your significant other. I'm not saying that I was right and he was wrong, but the problem was that we were going in two different directions. I know God kept telling me, "Daughter, this is not your husband," but I just wanted to get over my ex and live my life. I continued this unhealthy relationship in spite of what I was feeling in my gut.

I was also dealing with drama at work, and I didn't want to face any of my issues. I figured this guy would distract me and take the pain away. I kept asking God why He would promote me to a managerial role then have me to deal with all this drama. I was like, "Really, God, don't you think removing my ex out of my life was enough for now?" I asked God what I ever did do to deserve such things. I know, I was being so petty! Thank God for His grace and mercy, and for not listening to my nonsense. But the truth is, the majority of us do this "play the victim card," which, by the way, is not real faith. I was pretending to be happy externally, while internally I was so hurt and empty. I was tired and didn't know my purpose anymore, in any area of my life.

I felt like God was trying to punish me by not giving me love. I stayed with this guy for eleven months, even through all the arguments and tears. I stayed because I was afraid of being by myself.

I had to be honest about why I kept putting myself in destructive relationships. We women may not call them destructive because we find ways to justify the behavior. The small voice was starting to get louder and louder: "This is not your husband." I've learned that God is continually giving us instructions. We instead have a man whose beliefs and values are the opposite of ours because we are so afraid of being by ourselves.

How sad is this? We don't think God, who created everything and everyone, can actually bring us true love. We then go ahead of Him to develop more destructive behaviors. You know, God will allow us to continue going in this crazy circle until one day, hopefully, you will see the light and wake the heck up. Unfortunately, I still know of many women, even in their late thirties, forties, fifties, and sixties going through this vicious cycle. All because they are living in the lack mentality. Somehow, they have fooled themselves into thinking there are not enough men, or there's no such thing as a good man, so they keep up this disastrous performance.

This is why it's so imperative to make sure you keep your thoughts clean and surrender everything to God. You will end up single and bitter if you continue thinking this way. Yes, there are some abhorrent men, but there are also some prodigious God-fearing men in this world. There's a lot to be said about women, too. There's good and evil in both sexes. Please don't make this mistake of dating someone who you know is not for you because you are afraid you won't be able to find someone else better. I'm here to tell you, this is furthest from the truth. God wants to give us true love ordained by Him, but we can't have this unless we first seek God and love ourselves. You have to believe that God will never put you in a relationship where you will get hurt. We are the ones who ignore Him to only get hurt and realize He was right. Lack of faith will get you to believe such craziness.

Sometimes, some of our own beliefs stem from our upbringing and past adult experiences. Trust me; it was hard facing myself every day. I knew I deserved better and I knew what I was hearing from God, but ignored everything my intuition was telling me. I didn't know if I could trust it. I'm here to tell you that you can believe in your gut and the Holy Spirit one hundred percent. It's how you know right from wrong. I was still learning this and kept asking God how to know if it was Him. I even asked a few of my girlfriends, and none of them ever experienced what I was experiencing spiritually. Or was it because so many like myself were just starting to awaken and for so long had ignored the very gift God gave us: intuition.

Meanwhile, everything with my ex was going great. He was traded to another basketball team, which would later win two championship rings. He was forming a new sense of confidence that I never saw when we were together. I was starting to feel resentful. You see, when I was with my ex, teams swapped him amongst nine different basketball organizations. I had his back in his darkest moments, and now that we were not together, it seemed like everything in his life was shining.

Don't get me wrong, I was extremely happy for him, but I wasn't happy with how it was all unfolding. I was questioning God even more. "Lord, if you love me so much, then why does it seem like he's having all his dreams manifest, while you have me in this rut? What exactly have I done to you?" I was questioning my faith and all that I had learned so far. I felt like I was fooling myself in thinking that God was going to answer my prayers when it came to my love life. I was depressed and wanted nothing to do with listening to my inner spirit voice. I was letting my mind control me, feeling lost and confused about the path God had me on. I came to understand what it felt like when the voice within is telling you one thing, but the physical realm is manifesting the opposite. What do you do?

I will tell you what to do while you are waiting on God to reveal the answers you have been seeking— "You let go and let God." What I mean is that you focus on what God has you doing at this present moment. Understand that while you are waiting on God, distractions in your life will pop up. The enemy likes to confuse you or sadden your spirit. Remember, he came to steal, kill, and destroy. You have to be cognizant of your decision-making while you are waiting for God to show you what you have to do next. I will give you a perfect example.

An ex I had twelve years ago resurfaced. I was having dinner with one of my friends when he texted me; he had the habit of sending me random text messages every so often. This particular ex was probably my real first heartbreak in my early twenties. I used to pray to God all the time to please allow this man to change his cheating behavior. When you are young and dealing with a ton of insecurities, you tend to think it's you and not the other person. I learned that this couldn't be farther from the truth. When people hurt you, it has nothing to do with you but with the person's own demons and insecurities.

Anyhow, he popped into the restaurant where my friend and I were having dinner. It was very bizarre; I hadn't seen him in years. This was the man I was crazy in love with, or at least that's how I had felt twelve years before. In the past I would take him back over and over again, until one day I woke up told myself I couldn't do it anymore.

Now, twelve years later, I felt absolutely nothing. I forgave him for all the past pain, and most importantly, I excused myself for allowing him to do what he did to me. As I was looking at him, I heard a still, soft voice within whispering to me, "This is not your husband." Even then, I questioned the voice. I was trying to feel something for him because he had matured and was ready to settle down, but I couldn't deny what I felt. It felt so liberating to see how far I'd come and grown.

I had a moment in the restaurant when I came to an understanding of why God never allowed him to stop cheating on me. I could see how he would've never fit into the other chapters of my book (life). Of course, it was hard to decipher any of it twelve years ago. He would have stopped my growth into the woman God created me to be. I felt so delivered and grateful to Jesus Christ for not answering my prayer in the way that I had asked Him to!

God is constantly watching over us. He knows the beginning and the end of each of our lives. He knew this particular ex wouldn't fit into the next chapters of my book. I'd evolved so much since then. Here I was, twelve years later with a lot more confidence in who I was in Christ. I found myself at that very moment reflecting on God's goodness. My ex just kept talking, and since I had no interest in what he was saying, all I heard was, "Blah blah blah." I was in such disbelief about the fact I felt nothing for him. Ladies, trust what God is doing in your life. I couldn't make sense of it twelve years before, but now I could. I was sitting next to an ex who once upon a time I was genuinely in love with, who was pouring his heart out and apologizing for all the agonizing pain he caused me when we were together, and I felt nothing. I had a blank face while scratching my head trying to remember what exactly he did. God healed me and erased many of the hurtful events with him. I appreciated his apology, but I was in a new season that didn't include him. I was no longer the woman I was when I was with him, and our chapter had ended years ago.

Time does heal everything if you are willing to embrace God and go through whatever it is He needs you to do. He will mend your heart. It doesn't mean He will bring your soulmate right away; it just means He will heal you. Sometimes God needs to keep you in an isolated place to work on you. This is the only way He can bring out what he's called you to do; isolation forced upon us is where we indeed grow and heal our broken hearts. Another man will not cure your brokenness; only God can heal your heart.

Yes, of course, it gets very silent at times, and it can be a bit nerve-wracking. You see nothing happening. You've been on this journey for a while, or at least that's how you feel, and you're wondering if anything will ever change. I've been in this space, as well.

So, what do you do in the silent seasons? Get closer to God. You are still in the growing season. Pass the test! Don't go taking matters in your own hands by going out with men from your past, trying to meet someone new, or asking advice from your girlfriends who honestly don't have the slightest clue about what they are doing in their own lives. Trust God is with you, He's just working behind the scenes. He will bring forth the desires of your heart at the perfect time. I know you feel the timing is perfect now. Well, it's not . . . If it were, you wouldn't be feeling lonely or desperate to be in a relationship.

When you are whole, the loneliness and void are no longer in your heart. You know 100 percent the right person is coming, and until then you are living life. You are no longer consumed with concern over whether you will ever get married or, even worse, going to places in hopes that you will meet someone and go home saddened when it doesn't happen. The void can only be filled by God. It's a feeling that I can't explain, but trust me, you will know. When you get to this place, men will start flocking in, but you will be so complete that you'll be able to quickly decipher right away if the guy is supposed to be in your life or not. You won't fall just into anyone's arms. It will be uncomfortable and you will have many questionable moments, but keep pushing through, no matter what!

Trust that silence doesn't mean your prayers aren't being answered; it's life telling you it has a little more for you to go through to help you grow. The growth you are undertaking is a must for the next level of your life. Go through it so you won't have to continue taking the same test over and over again.

I remember one specific day I found myself feeling so lonely and hearing nothing from God. I was struggling with deep thoughts and decided to take a run on the beach. The ocean helps me reconnect with my true essence. It was an incredible run. I found myself feeling good again, until one negative thought slipped into my mind. All of a sudden, my forty-five-minute run was ruined by the craziness I had created in my head. We have to take control of our negative slip-ups. It is crazy how one lousy thought can create another horrible theory, and so on. It will turn your entire day gloomy. You can literally create a whole movie in your head; all you need is some good ole popcorn and soda and there goes your drama movie. Ladies, we can go from being so confident in God answering our prayers to letting our minds take over with foolishness within a split second.

A week after the run, five guys contacted me. Three of the guys I'd dealt with in the past, and two were relatively new. I had a quick thought: Why does it even matter if all these guys hit me up if God already said they were not the one? Was my ego involved? Was the good feeling coming from a place of men or God? But then I paused and had a moment to myself. If God already revealed the truth about the five guys, why not pass the test and keep it moving along?

You have to have self-talks and encourage yourself to keep going. I didn't want to waste time with idiocy. I decided not to answer any of them—I knew what I wanted. I'd already prayed to God to give me peace and to know when one arrived. I wasn't getting those feelings from any of the five; I decided to trust my gut.

I do believe we have to be in a place of wholeness to be able to love someone else. An area of wholeness never looks for anything or anyone from the outside to bring them joy; it exists as it is.

Listen, I knew these things, yet I found myself falling short at times. It's all human behavior and more of a reason you need to seek God before men. God will give us the strength required to make wiser decisions; in return, we won't compromise our happiness for a short-term gratification due to solitude or fear. We all go through this loneliness for a period.

I have a friend who was very successful in her career but was very unhappy with her love life. She was dealing with a guy younger than her for some time, but things between the two of them were not getting any better. Here's the kicker: he told her from the beginning he wasn't looking to be in a serious relationship because he was focusing on his "career." Ladies, red flag, red flag, and some more red flag! Yes, I do agree men usually don't like to settle down when they are chasing after their careers, but I also know that when they want someone, nothing will stop them from pursuing her.

When you hear a man say he's not ready to be in a serious relationship, believe him. Don't go thinking wild sex or being there for him will get him to change his mind. It will make the matter even worse—he will lose respect for you. Why would he value you when you don't see your worth? Men are usually very honest about what they want. When in doubt, watch his actions; they will tell you if he's seeking a monogamous relationship.

This is why God says, "Be still and know that I am God" in Psalm 46:10. I know we will have moments when we feel conflicted about where God is taking us, especially in our love lives. You can't force a man to be in a relationship or marriage. You have to pray and ask God what you should do. If he's not the husband He's ordained for you, Jesus will remove him.

Every time I've prayed this powerful prayer, "Lord, if this is not the man you have ordained to be my husband, please release him from me," somehow the guy vanishes. It became very comical, to the point I used to tell God, "Okay, Lord, can I at least get a dinner date and some conversation before you remove him?" Again, God does hear us; you can keep it one hundred with Him. He knows what you are thinking and feeling anyways.

In my teens and twenties, the men I dated stayed around—or I kept them around—because I didn't have a deep relationship with God. I never asked God before dating a guy if he was supposed to be in my life. I didn't understand the power of prayers and knew nothing about the Bible. And it wasn't because God didn't want to have a relationship with me—God's love for me has never changed from the moment He created me. His love remains the same forever. I wasn't trying to get too close to Him. I knew deep inside some of the things I was doing weren't cool with the Lord. He wouldn't condone my lifestyle. I knew Jesus existed, and even attended church on Sundays, but I was still lost. I was trying to find love in all the wrong places.

I went through so many unnecessary heartbreaks—if I knew then what I know now, I would have never entered many of those relationships. I have no idea how I made it so long with a lukewarm relationship with God. God doesn't deal well with lukewarm people. He either wants you in or out. For the word says in Revelation 3:16, "So, because you are lukewarm—neither hot nor cold—I am about to spit you out of my mouth." Ouch, right? But I get it now.

Do you like flaky people? How would you feel if someone loved you one day, but the next day he didn't? You would probably want the person to decide if they were in or out. That's exactly what God wants from us. We have to make a decision. Are we going to live God's way or not? He gives us free will, so the choice is optimally ours. But let it be known, if you choose to do things your way, it will bring a lot of sorrow and darkness. You may experience temporary or false happiness, but it's only a matter of time before your life will come crashing down, and you may even wonder if it's worth living anymore.

We see it regularly in the entertainment business. Many of us were wondering why a particular woman celebrity is going through all that drama when she's so beautiful and successful. Could it be that she doesn't have God in the center of her life? I can't begin to tell you, living God's way is the best decision I've ever made. It's a joy that no one can take away. I love everything about me. There's a feeling of peace within me that genuinely surpasses my human understanding.

Take ten minutes to reevaluate your love life. Is there a man you are dating that you're unsure about? You can sense it in your spirit but you're still a bit confused on which direction to go in. Write down all the pros and cons. Once you've jotted these down, if you realize this person is not for you, I want you to take five to ten minutes to talk to God about what you truly want and the sacrifices you are willing to make to have your prayers answered. This does mean letting go of the person and trusting God has heard your prayers. He will bring you the desires of your heart in His perfect timing. ARE YOU READY???

Pros	Cons

I learned from Tony Robbins, Date with Destiny that men and women go into relationships with their own expectations and never discuss them with their partner. It's imperative to have a list of your relationship goals, and I couldn't agree more. It's so important to know what you want in a relationship.

One major reason we end up with men not aligned with who we are at our core is that we are not intentional. If you don't know entirely what you are looking for in a soulmate, you are going to attract a man who is not for you. Sometimes we date from a lonely place and somehow convince ourselves he's a good catch, only to find out down the road that you two couldn't be any more different. Now you've wasted precious time, which would have been put to better use with someone designed for you. I've done this many times in my life. I squandered many of my years with men who I knew deep in my heart weren't the one.

To help you out, I've shared what my relationship goals are:

1. God-fearing man

2. Loving

3. Successful

4. Peaceful

5. Great communicator

6. Affectionate

7. Wants to get married

8. Wants to have a minimum of two kids

9. Enjoys traveling

10. Enjoys hanging out with his family

Now it's your turn to write the ten "must-haves" for your relationship. Take a moment to think this through. What are your top ten?

1. _____

2. _____

3. _____

4. _____

5. _____

6. _____

7. _____

8. _____

9. _____

10. _____

CHAPTER THREE

DISAPPOINTMENTS WILL HELP YOU GROW

Disappointment and setbacks are all part of the process. Specific situations will happen in your life that you will have no control over. These instances are not permanent setbacks; they're set up to put you in a winning position. Are you wondering what you should do while you are in a setback? Plant your feet and stand firm. Don't try to rush or skip the difficult times; you will miss a pivotal part of the journey.

During the distress, you will encounter loneliness, loss, boredom, confusion, doubts, and fear. All of these emotions are absolutely normal, but you can't let them take over you. The breakups and the men you dated who walked away were all part of your growth. They weren't supposed to be part of your grand finale for this season. Don't judge yourself for where you are in life right now. You will be assessing too prematurely and miss out on the greater picture.

There was a stage in my life when everything seemed to be getting worse. I found out the ex who I had dated for four years was having a baby, and within the same week, I was diagnosed with a tumor. I called my sister, crying uncontrollably, not understanding why it all was occurring at the same time. I perceived my universe to be collapsing. I sat in the sanctuary I built in my room and wept for days. I repeatedly kept saying, "God, I know this didn't catch you by surprise, but I need your help. I have no idea where to turn or how to hear your voice to know how to follow the path you have set before me."

I am sharing my story to let you know that trials and tribulations don't skip anyone. We all go through some hardships. Can you imagine doctors telling you they will have to remove five teeth in order to remove a tumor from your face? Yes, it was hard, but it also pushed me even harder to keep pressing forward. When I felt abandoned and lost, I would go to my sanctuary in my room and speak to God, and if I was at work I would go to the bathroom. I asked God to please renew my strength, mind, and spirit.

I felt there had to be a reason why all this was transpiring at the same time. I kept telling myself, "Angelina, you will surpass this. You are strong, courageous, determined, and you will come out winning." You have to encourage yourself! If you say this daily a few times out loud, your mind will start believing it and you will begin to have a more positive attitude.

The hindrances were all happening while I was writing this book—my spirit was so weakened, I started to procrastinate every night and abandoned my writing. But these hurdles were just distractions from the dark side to keep me away from pursuing my goal. I was having profoundly troubling thoughts, but I just kept talking and comforting myself. I had no control over what was happening, but I did have the power to decide how I was going to handle this time in my life.

It was all necessary to get me where I am today. Sometimes it sucks when you are going through the growing process. It feels like you are being ripped to shreds. During my trial season, I prayed like I never had before. The first time I saw the aftermath of my surgery, it felt like someone punched me in my stomach. I felt so abandoned, lost, and confused; while asking God, "Why is this all happening to me when I've been faithful?" I looked up at my bathroom ceiling and wondered when it all was going to come to an end.

For eight months I had sleepless nights with my pillow soaked in tears. I felt at the time that all I was experiencing was disappointment after disappointment. Every time I felt like I was giving up on my faith, I couldn't help but look around me to see how God has blessed me in so many ways. I knew there was no way He would leave me in this place. I knew this season was designed to build a sturdier me, a woman of great faith who could overcome whatever life threw at her. I was determined to continue pressing forward.

As we know by now, life can be perplexing. A few weeks later, three different guys were trying to get my attention. I wasn't sure what to do, so I asked God to please let me know if I should be talking to any of them. Based in where I was in life, it was safe to say I shouldn't be talking to anyone. I had some serious healing to do, but I chose to do things my way.

I ended up reaching back out to one of them, and I was so disappointed with his behavior. Are you surprised? I totally went ahead of God. It seemed like everything revolved around this new guy. Interestingly enough, I felt it from the first discussion we had over the phone—a sign I completely disregarded. I was trying to look beyond his faults by justifying it with "no one is perfect." It's true, no one is perfect, but being imperfect should be "he's a little messy," or "he gets quiet at times for no reason."

We shouldn't excuse the conduct of men by thinking it is okay if he only calls you once a week, or that he doesn't keep his word, or by compromising your values to try to keep him around. Ladies, these are not God's ways. God loves us too much to give us a half of a man.

Be patient and be okay with being single while God is preparing your husband for you.

Anyhow, we spoke on the phone a few more times and texted, but after a month and a half, I realized this man was not trying to get to know me. A man trying to get to know me for all the right reasons would be pursuing me. He would want to contact me on a regular basis and ask me tons of questions, and I wasn't getting any of this from him. I've learned by now that if it walks and talks like a duck, it's a duck.

God was showing me all along, and I refused to see the obvious. Yes, he texted me every day, but I almost felt like I was part of his to-do list. He would text me and then when I responded, he wouldn't answer back. When I went into my prayer closet about my situation, I just kept hearing, "Daughter, he's not the one." I couldn't ignore what I was hearing from God. I had to listen and see how it would all unfold.

Ladies, things don't just happen. They occur to help us grow and learn from our mistakes. I'm providing you a close-up of some past situations just in case you are on this pathway or it presents itself shortly. Continue telling yourself, "God has me and I'm trusting the process." A heaviness comes off of us the moment we decide to do things God's way. We may not know what that fully entails, but I believe it means staying in the present moment and giving your best while appreciating the journey.

At my saddest and most fearful moments, God has revealed to me who He is. I'm discovering attributes about myself that I never knew: The good, the bad, the things I need to work on, the things I need to let go of, and things I just need to stand still on. It's interesting how He will use our darkest hours to reveal our light. You have to know God is our Father and He knows the beginning and the end. He knows exactly how everything is going to develop. We have to be determined each day to learn how to discern God's voice more and more. We can't do this walk on our own. Every time I made a choice based on emotions, it took me backwards.

We may not ever know why certain doors closed, but I do know it's part of the journey to bring us to a moment in life when one day it just clicks. You will reflect on how far you've come and how who you are becoming is so much better than who you were. If the ex didn't walk away, you would not be the person you are today. He would have hindered your growth. It would have been impossible to move to your next chapter.

This is the main reason why you see some people who are stagnant. They refuse to let go of the people and things God is trying to remove. He's only interested in giving us our very best. Why not let go of what you think you want or need? Have confidence that He has something so much better for you. There is hope in dark moments. Those dark points build character, strength, clarity, and wisdom for the next period of your walk.

We try to have our lives scripted out with all of the extravagant details, and when things don't go as planned, we go ballistic. I hope you know by now that God is the only one who knows every aspect of your life. The bigger the calling, the more hurdles you will have to jump. God may give you a glimpse of what He's doing, but many times He won't. If you are not careful, you will allow quiet seasons to define who you are and where you are going. You need to suck it up, pull your big girl panties on, and do whatever is necessary to push through the hurt and pain. There's something inside of you that you need to birth. You are pregnant with your purpose right now; let it take its natural development. Somehow, all the confusion, tears, hurt, and whatever else you may be feeling will work out in your best interest.

This book would've never been birthed if it wasn't for my ex walking away. God put a firm conviction in my heart about writing. I tried to run away from the calling because I'm extremely private about my life, but I knew I needed to be obedient. It was hard being open about who I've dated and what I've experienced over the past four years. You can't deny the strong feeling deep inside your stomach when God is requesting that you complete an assignment.

When the emotions would arise in my soul, I would write. I would reread some of my chapters; I felt lights in my heart being turned on. Oh, how grateful I was that God did what He did with me. I was incredibly thankful for the man who walked away, the man I was sincerely in love with and who I thought would be my husband. I was so grateful, and I never looked back.

The secret to being happy is to accept where God has you. We tend to want to rush the process or get offended when we are not where we expected to be at a certain age. A few of my single, beautiful girlfriends question why they are single, have even lost hope about whether they will ever find a good man. They question if God is real, and if He is, why does He have them in this predicament?

It's demented to allow ourselves to fall into this trap. Do you really think God wants us unhappy or single for the rest of our lives? Absolutely not. God has you in a dry place for a particular reason. Sometimes we keep our negative attitudes and disorderly behavior for longer than God anticipated.

I used to be this person, only to come to a place of sadness and hollowness. I made a conscious decision to do something about it; in addition to going to church and reading my Bible, I started reading self-help books, attending conferences, and listening to the best coaches in the game about "Becoming the best you." One principle with everyone I listened to was the importance of gratitude. Are you wondering why being in a grateful mindset is so imperative? It returns your spirit back to a place of joy and peace. You start noticing all the blessings God has poured into your life thus far, and this will give you strength to keep going because you know more great stuff is coming.

For example, you have a great family and friends who love you immensely, you have a roof over your head—the list can go on and on. I suggest you take a few minutes before going to sleep to journal down ten things that went well throughout your day. This allows your desires to manifest a lot quicker. When you are moaning and grumbling about your singleness and loneliness, this negative energy creates more of what you don't want.

You have to sense God is on your side. He will bring forth all of the hopes of your heart. You have to let go of what's not happening for you and center your attention on all the good that is taking place. I'm pretty sure if you took a minute to list five to ten blessings right now, you would find yourself saying, "Life is not bad at all; I'm blessed."

Let's take a few minutes to list all the great things that are happening for you in this moment.

1. _____
2. _____
3. _____
4. _____
5. _____
6. _____
7. _____
8. _____
9. _____
10. _____

Now, take a few seconds to breathe in all the great things happening in your life in this present moment. We focus so much on the inadequacies of our lives that we forget to pay attention to our spectacular surroundings. God is great! He has done many great things in your life.

When you find yourself going down a slippery slope, pause for a second and refocus. It's so crucial to surround yourself with people who speak positivity, who can hold you accountable when you are reverting to your old ways. But ultimately, this is your life; you have to manage it accordingly. You have to know that no matter how bad it seems, God will bring the promise to pass.

Please remind yourself that God removed your ex, or the guys you were talking to vanished on purpose. He may or may not reveal to you why the relationship came to a standstill; your job is to have certainty that it's for an excellent reason. The more you allow your brain to think of all the memories you two shared, the longer it's going to take for you to get to the point of surrender. When you find yourself getting discontented, you've allowed your thoughts to take over. Your mind doesn't know the future—you are the one creating a narrative that may never happen.

Imagine yourself jumping from a 50th floor building. Did your heart stop? Did you get afraid? Of course you did, but it never even happened. It's the same concept: if you allow yourself to go back to your past, you will create unnecessary pain for yourself. Remember, God doesn't make any errors. Your future is better than your history. You can plan all you want, but it's ultimately up to God to let your plan flourish. For it says in Proverbs 19:21, "Many are the plans in a person's heart, but it is the LORD's purpose that prevails."

I stated I thought I would be marrying my ex, but God had a bigger plan for me. I didn't see it at the moment. Psalm 86:11, an exemplary scripture to recite when you are tempted to do things your way, says, "Teach me your way, LORD, that I may rely on your fruitiness; give me an undivided heart, that I may fear your name." Another great scripture to read as soon as you open your eyes is Psalms 143:8, which teaches, "Let me hear of your unfailing love each morning, for I am trusting you. Show me where to walk, for I give myself to you."

If you don't govern your thoughts early in the morning, they will control your whole day. Train yourself to pause when you start thinking about foolishness that is not empowering you. You have absolute power over your thinking. If you find your feelings racing toward negativity, stop where you are and say a quick prayer, "Jesus Christ, please take control of my thoughts and renew them with yours," or quote the scripture above.

Many of the self-development and empowering books indicate the importance of controlling your thinking. People who can overcome many setbacks in their lives are the ones who were able to say no to their negative thinking and yes to empowering self-talk. It's okay to have small conversations with yourself, even if they're out loud and people think you're crazy. Whatever it takes and whatever works for you—do it. Maybe also getting a journal to write down your perceptions so you can go back to see how pessimistic your brain can be when you are the one allowing it to do what it wants. It is a conscious decision.

Again, I could've let my ex-boyfriend's achievements drive me to depression, but I understood if God wanted me with him, He would've kept the relationship going or brought him back. I chose not to dwell on the past. When I reflected on our relationship on a deeper level, I'm not sure my current level of maturity would've worked with him. Staying with him would have prevented my mental growth, derailed all I have accomplished thus far, and most importantly, stopped me from becoming the woman I became when he walked away.

Say, "Thank you for walking away!"

CHAPTER FOUR

DON'T GIVE UP

There will be desperate moments in our lives when we feel as though the pain is never going to leave and we start losing hope. We will try to become better and believe there's a reason for everything, but it just feels easier to give up. We pray, read self-help books, and maybe start going back to church, but nothing is helping to expedite the healing process. You're trying your very best to lean on God, but for whatever reason you can't find the strength or even know how to get back to the feeling of joy.

In this journey of finding yourself, you have to be strong and courageous and never give up, no matter how hard it is. The moments of defeat are building character and substance. Yes, it's easy to lose faith in your dream and get deflated by current affairs. I also had my moments of distress when I'd been praying for a husband, and a guy would show up and turn out to be different from what I expected.

I would get upset and despondent, especially when I'd been praying for it for so long. I found myself not having the energy to pray, but even when I didn't feel like it I would just open my mouth and start praying and crying to God to give me the muscles to keep moving onward. In times of defeatism, you are developing character and substance. Yes, it's easy to lose faith in your dreams and get deflated by current affairs. I even had some days where I didn't even have the stamina to pray. But it was in those moments that I forced myself to have a conversation with God about whether I was really doing this whole "faith" walk.

Set aside dedicated quality time to spend with God. I prefer it to be first thing in the morning. As soon as I get out of bed, I go to an area that's quiet and have a one on one with God. 1 John 5:14 says, "This is the confidence we have in approaching God: that if we ask anything according to his will, he hears us." This particular time with God is so essential to our spiritual growth—can you imagine starting a job without any training or instructions? You would be lost, never knowing what your job duties or top priorities were and probably doing a whole lot of busy work.

This is precisely what happens when we don't spend time with God. You can have a candid conversation with Him; He will give you instructions on what you need to do. It also gives you a powerful jumpstart in your day! You are starting the day with the 'One' who already knows how it's all going to unfold; you are just asking Him to show you the way. Remember, this journey is taking one action at a time. You can't try to foresee your entire future based on the chapter you are in presently. Our thoughts are based on past occurrences and what we assume our futures will be. The only one who knows the future is Jesus Christ. You are only responsible for walking into what the present moment has to offer you. You can figure out quickly if you are on the right path or not if you stop to see whether the task at hand is leading you in the direction you want to go.

Let me give you an example: let's say you are talking to a guy, but he's not entirely up to par with your core values. He's not the most

Godly man, he's not consistent with his phone calls or text messages and only seems to reach out at random moments, his actions are not matching his words, and you realize you are not feeling 100 percent secure on how he's making you feel. This will not lead you to the route you are praying for.

This means you will have to cut him off immediately. But I'm guessing you are wondering if this will leave you single again. Yes, it will. But why would you want half of a man anyways? Make sure your actions are aligning with what you are praying for. Don't compromise with a short-term gratification for a long-term promise. Don't do it, ladies! Finding the time with God first thing in the morning before the world awakens is going to help you make some really powerful decisions for your life. God will speak to your heart. Yes, it will require making some really tough commitments, but it will be worth the wait.

You have the sturdiness within you to keep doing what you need to do for this chapter in your life. Your nervous system will make you feel like you are making the worst decision in your life, but let me reassure you that your dream will come to pass when it is a God-given desire. Isaiah 30:21 says, "And your ears shall hear a word behind you, saying, 'This is the way, walk in it,' when you turn to the right or when you turn to the left." He will guide you on the path He designed specifically for you. Don't be afraid to listen to what the Holy Spirit is asking you to do.

I've made many tough choices, and some were easier than others, but nevertheless, they all led me on this path that allowed me to become the woman I am today. The difficult decisions are usually the ones that will provide the next opportunity.

I stand on this scripture when I find myself unsure where my life is taking me. Proverbs 3:5-6 teaches, "Trust in the Lord with all your heart, and do not lean on your own understanding. In all your ways acknowledge him, and he will make straight your paths." Do not lean to your own understanding. Your mind will always try to rationalize everything. The Creator of this universe doesn't do things from a sensible viewpoint; if He did, He wouldn't be God. Seriously, can you even make sense of how this universe was created, meaning everything and everyone in it? Of course not, so why try to discern what God is doing in your life? Stop attempting to do God's job, and trust me when I tell you He doesn't need your assistance. Your duty is to take the next step forward.

Women make a mistake when meeting a man who piques their interest: they automatically picture him as their husband. Stop it, ladies; please stop it. God sits high and looks low, and God does not send every man that comes your way. Morning prayers will allow you to decipher the imposters from the real thing. Connecting back to your true self will get you aligned with what God has in store for you and only you. No one can take him from you, he will not pass you by, and he's not yet passed you.

I used to think maybe my strong personality turned "the one" for me away, or perhaps "the one" was already taken. I know, what kind of insane person would think of such things? And, the answer is us, ladies. If we don't commit first thing in the morning with God, we will create fictional stories in our heads. Ask Him to take full control of your day, thoughts, heart, and spirit. Ask Him to show you the way.

Prayer:

My Lord, I come to you this morning asking you to direct each step I take through the entire day. I invite you to renew my strength, mind, and spirit. Let me surrender the desires of my heart to you this morning and focus on what exactly you need me to do. Transform me into the woman you designed me to be.

Thank you for working with me so I can be the wife I need to be to the husband you have ordained for me. I refuse to go ahead of you this time. I will patiently wait for you, Jesus Christ. I know I am love. I already have everything I need at this present moment because I have you. When I get afraid about my future, I will stand on your word in Isaiah 41:14: "For I am the LORD your God who takes hold of your right hand and says to you, do not fear; I will help you." Thank you for who I am and becoming. I pray this in Jesus Christ's name, Amen.

Recite this prayer every morning until you are comfortable enough to say your own prayer.

While you are on this new journey, people who you used to date or even just friends you used to hang with will start popping up back in your life. Stand your ground and remember that this is a race and you are refusing to quit halfway. You need to keep yourself fueled with daily scriptures, so if the past is showing up in the moment of despair, you won't have the urge to respond back. Now that you have been working on yourself, you know what your core values are and you've asked God to bring these things forth. What come next are distractions. Sometimes life is testing us to see how committed we are on this path.

Don't let all the training and self-improvement go to waste for one moment of gratification. You have to finish strong, and don't get sidetracked by things or people who have shown you they are on a different path. Only a healthy mind can walk away or refuse to reply. It takes strength to say, "I will not settle, I will get what I want, or even better." Remind yourself that you have everything it takes within you to complete this chapter of your life as a winner. You will be able to share these lessons with others who are currently going through what you've gone through to give them the courage to keep stretching.

Standing your ground comes with very lonely moments, but these moments are building more and more character. You are going to look back when you cross the finish line and feel so proud of all the endurance you developed within yourself to complete the race. You are a stronger you, a better you.

Don't get weak. Don't come this far to stay here; stand your ground and let God, the Creator of everything and everyone, know that you are serious about this walk and serious about what you want in life. You don't care what it takes or how many hurdles you have to jump through, you will do what is necessary to receive blessings. Nothing in life worth having is easy. If it comes easy, it will also leave easy.

Don't let anyone ever treat you like you are second class. You are magnificent and perfectly made. If a man can't see it from the jump, then he's not worth keeping around. Walk away with your head high and ladylike; remember, you are a representation of The Most High. There's no need to ridicule yourself by posting degrading pictures on the internet to show him what he's missing out on; silence is golden. You walk away and stand your ground in what you want out of life.

Continue empowering yourself by spending time with God. You will feel great because you let that imposter go and you are now closer to receiving your husband. The quicker you can tell the imposters from the real thing, the easier the journey gets. You will be able to spot the fakers from a mile away. When you get to the point that you know who you are in Christ, they will know you are different. They will be forced to walk away without even having a valid reason why. This is called God's protection.

The closer you get to God, the more you will have a hedge of protection over you. They will flee so fast it will make your head spin. Please, ladies, do not take it personally when God starts removing them quickly. Nope, it's not you. There's nothing wrong that you need to fix to make him stay. God is removing the men who are not part of His divine plan for you.

Too many times I see women trying to enhance their looks, thinking there's something wrong with them. It saddens my heart because they are telling God He made a mistake when He created them. And we all know God doesn't make any mistakes, but if you didn't know, let me tell you what the Word says in Luke 12:7: "Even every hair on your head has been counted. Don't be afraid!" Every hair on your head has been counted, which means God created you so thoroughly that He even knew how much hair He was going to give you. I don't know about you, but that alone gives me goosebumps. He has a plan for each one of us. He knows when He will bring you your husband, and who he is. You should be able to rest in peace just knowing this truth.

Don't try to improve what is already perfect, especially for someone God didn't intend to be part of your life. Look at yourself in the mirror and repeat to yourself that you are beautiful, confident, perfectly made in God's image, intelligent, and God-fearing. Thank God for whatever he's blocking instead of feeling like he's trying to hurt you or punish you. James 1:2, says, "God blesses those who patiently endure testing and temptation. Afterward, they will receive the crown of life that God has promised to those who love him."

Pass the test of trials and tribulations. The test comes in different forms, but you will know when it's a life test. Pass it so you can receive the crown of life. Not loving yourself or thinking you are not pretty enough, not skinny enough, your butt is not big enough, or whatever other complexities you may be dealing with, is another form of saying God didn't know what He was doing when He created you. Girlfriends, please hear the words coming out of my mouth: The guys didn't leave you because you weren't enough, they left you because God allowed it. He knows you would have been settling for less than His best.

The moment you decided to put God first, He went to work. Spend time with God; He will lead the way, and you will see your worth and value. I can't even express the confidence I have in me. It's not arrogant or boastful, but it's just a knowing feeling of who I am, and since God created me and composed me with a specific look and purpose, then I must be real fly; there's not another me out there.

In moments when any insecurities kick in, I quickly remind myself how perfectly made I am and that there's not another me in this entire universe.

Now, let's forget about our past as we are reminded to do in Philippians 3:13: "Brothers, I do not consider myself to have taken hold of it. But one thing indeed: Forgetting the things behind and reaching forward to the things ahead." We got it going on, my spiritual sisters, we do. I hope you are starting to feel good about the direction you are headed in. Feel certain that you are beginning to let go of every rejection that caused you hurt and pain. You are stepping boldly into the present with a new attitude and standing your ground to see the desires of your heart come to pass. You are going to look in the mirror every day to remind yourself how beautiful you are and how God created one remarkable human being. You are going to allocate quality time with God every morning, before starting your day, to get God's instructions for what is ahead of you. You will not get derailed by your past or any distractions that may be pulling you away from your deepest desires.

You are a phenomenal woman, remember that!

I decided that no matter how much pain I was in, I had to push through. It was the best decision I ever made. This book I'm writing wouldn't be occurring if it wasn't for my heartbreak. This is why, again,

I believe everything happens for a reason. You have to trust the process; it may be the very thing that will push you to your life's purpose.

People who know me always hear me say, "Don't touch it." It's precisely how I maneuver through life. I understand when hurtful events happen, which they will, that none of them have caught God by surprise. It doesn't mean I'm not hurting, it just means I'm trusting the process of life. I accept things are unfolding just the way they should.

In such an instantly gratified and emotional society, we tend to want to control and fix things quickly and in our own way. This is how you miss your blessings. God could have something so much bigger and better down the road, but since we can't see it, we tend to want to take the shortcut. The most interesting element about this is that so many people are used to functioning on autopilot and so they aren't even aware of their behavior.

Jesus mentioned, "Peace I leave with you" three hundred sixty-five times in the Bible, which means He knew we would get worried and anxious about our problems every day. We don't need to go chasing after anyone who God allowed to walk out of our lives. If God wanted him to stay, He would have never allowed him to leave. You can't go saying, "I have faith" and do the opposite of what faith is. Trust me, I've already made the mistakes for you. You lose your value the moment you make the person feel like you can't live without them. You are idolizing him, and God is a jealous God. If you refuse to listen, God will let you have your way . . . but eventually it will fall apart, leaving you in a worse dilemma. Do yourself a favor, girlfriend, and LET IT GO! Dedicate your single life to God; figure out your passions before you meet your husband.

Adversities are all part of the growing pain, and they allow us to gain more wisdom and clarity. The day I found out about my tumor was the day I understood the real meaning of life—life is a gift.

Our darkest moments are when we find out who we are. Are you a victor or a victim? When my health was affected, I recognized it as another growing season, and if God allowed it, it must be something He was going to use to help others. If we don't resist it, it will be a monumental moment. The worst thing we can do is run to a vice to remove the pain.

There are numerous vices people lean on, such as another relationship, sex, alcohol, toxic friendships; the list goes on. Don't find yourself tripping on this stumbling block. It doesn't matter how uncomfortable it is; keep pressing forward.

We all have a calling on this Earth. You are uniquely made and came to serve a purpose. Remember, all your past hurting relationships, health issues, or dysfunctional upbringing help you become better and keep you evolving. This is why it disheartens me when I see women settle for less than God's best. They give up right before their breakthrough. Don't be that woman! Be a woman of courage and persistence. Don't give up in the midst of the battle! Some women are walking around thinking they are less than their partner or comparing themselves with other women. Oh my, this is one of the biggest mistakes you can make.

When you start comparing your life to others', you are missing out on who you are. Hopefully, it won't be too late to make the necessary changes. Too many times we ignore the fear factors; we are afraid of failing, or being judged by others, or being labeled as a failure. Life is way too valuable, and we have a limited time here on Earth to be compromising who we are to fit in. You weren't made to fit in; you are here to stand out and to leave a dent in the universe.

When times get tough, which they will, you have to find the deeper reason of why you even started this new adventure. The "why" will get you to push through the barriers. There's no such thing as a bad or good season. They are both being worked out to bring out your very best. You don't need to know all the details; you need to see yourself finishing the race. Do something each day to bring you closer to your vision. I know our dreams sometimes can scare us. They may seem way out of our reach, but if God gave you the mental image, you hold on tight to it and start taking actions towards it.

You have to step out on faith. Don't be afraid! You may or may not fail on the first try, but I've never seen a successful person not fail in the first round. It's all part of the process. I said this before: this book has been in my heart for a while now, but I doubted my ability to be an author. I didn't even know where to start. I decided to ignore what I felt my heart telling me until I couldn't ignore it any more, and I knew I had to get to work. I've experienced so much more than what I've written here, but this gives you an idea from where this book first stemmed. I found myself writing after work and on weekends. God was guiding me every step of the way.

If each of us looked in the mirror and asked ourselves, "Who am I truly behind this body, makeup, fashion, shoes, friends, lifestyle, etc.?" we would quickly learn that the person in front of the mirror is so much more than external factors. If you let go of all the fear or judgment of the world, you will also discover you have something to offer this universe that no one else can do but you.

CHAPTER FIVE

INSTINCTS

Too many times we go against our instincts. Our spirit knows things before they even happen. Jesus Christ lives in us and guides us, and one significant way is through the Holy Spirit, which takes the form of our gut. When your stomach feels like something is wrong—trust it. This is God guiding you.

Of course, the journey is not simple, but it's not supposed to be. A simple life is for people who are okay with mediocrity. Growth only occurs when we face our trials and tribulations and are willing to stick it out. I promise you; it can't happen in any other way.

You learn how to make wiser decisions when you stop rushing towards the first guy who is trying to offer you a relationship. You can take a step back to evaluate the situation and ask God if this is of Him.

What's cool about not rushing the process is that you learn so much about yourself. You can enjoy the ride and start living full out by enjoying your own presence. Go to the movies, dinner, happy hour, workshops, and travel by yourself. When you start enjoying your own company, you've come to a place of wholeness. How is anyone else going to enjoy your company when you can't even stand being with yourself? People treat you on the same level that you respect yourself. This is the reason you need to love yourself thoroughly first before asking God to bring someone into your life. You will screw it up, or even worse, you will attract a person who is as broken as you are.

In the midst of getting to know yourself, you also learn how to enjoy your life while waiting for God to answer your prayers. I love hanging out with my family, friends, traveling, and trying new adventures. It's also imperative to spend time with myself—reading a great book or going to the movies, and yes, this would be by myself. Be okay being alone and getting to know yourself with no one around. Hint: you need to love yourself thoroughly first before asking God to bring you someone into your life, because it helps you automatically raise your standards. Don't lower your standards or compromise who you are to have someone in your life. That's an insult to God and humanity.

There were specific behaviors I wasn't aware that I was doing until I started spending time with myself. The quiet seasons taught me the most. I avoided the alone time for a long while, maybe because I didn't want to face myself and wasn't ready to make the necessary changes. I tried to point fingers at my ex instead of looking at my solo time as a learning opportunity. The quiet times are not to torture you or to get you to think about all that's going wrong in your life; they exist to help you get to know your true self. If God did bring you the husband before you knew yourself, he still wouldn't complete you. Only God can fill the void. Once you are sufficiently complete, you will be able to love others from a loving place.

A place of isolation doesn't always feel good. We are yearning for companionship, but the issue is when you have the wrong companion. It's detrimental to your soul when you get impatient and end up with the wrong person, wasting precious years you can never get back. Waiting on God may not always feel gratifying, but it is the most rewarding and satisfying action you can ever take. You can look around to see how many unhappy and unfilled relationships are around. There are two ways relationships come about: by our flesh, or by God. The divorce rate is so high because people rush into marriage without first consulting with God to see if the union is supposed to happen. We ignore all the warning signs saying, "Don't marry him/her, fool." Now you are stuck in a marriage that you knew deep within your gut wasn't right for you.

God will let you jump in the fire. God is a loving God, and He will never force Himself on us. But what you can't do is play the victim when you get burned. He tells us the best route to go, but if we decide to take a shortcut, we are on our own until we call on God to help us. You need to know when God is giving you the green or the red light. Meditation, which I will discuss later on, will help you with making more precise and concise decisions. Remember, God is not a God of disorder.

If you are entering into a union that seems confusing, chaotic, and complicated, it's not of God. He created us and knew exactly how we could live a peaceful and joyful life, even when you are in the midst of a storm. We just like to take matters in our own hands. It took a lot of hard knocks to get my attention. Don't be this person; I'm trying to save you from the unnecessary heartbreaks or disappointments. God teaches me every day that He does have a master plan for every soul He brings to this Earth. Our duties are to ask Him to reveal this plan each step of the way; deep inside, you have all the answers. If we dare to try to calculate his every move, we will get afraid. Remember, we can't predict the future; we have to take it one day at a time. Ask Him each day what exactly He needs you to achieve throughout this day.

One of my favorite scriptures I read in the morning is in Psalm 5:1-3: "Listen to my words, Lord, consider my lament. Hear my cry for help, my King, and my God, for to you, I pray. In the morning, Lord, you hear my voice; in the morning I lay my requests before you and wait expectantly." This scripture soothes my heart. Did you see "wait expectantly?" Make your request to the Lord and wait for Him to answer. He may not answer you right away, but rest assured, He will answer. He will let you know which path to take. You can't be praying and still worrying. Trust your gut when you hear a voice within, especially when you are in the presence of God (praying), as this is another way of Him speaking to you.

What do you believe? Do you believe God will answer your prayers? Remember, there are certain types of maturity needed for each chapter you go into before God can answer your prayer for a husband. First Thessalonians 5:16-18 says, "Rejoice at all times. Pray without ceasing. Give thanks in every circumstance, for this is God's will for you in Christ Jesus." You can't stop praying or give up on your faith when nothing is happening, but in all circumstances give God thanks. There is a reason why He still has you waiting. You may not like it, and you may even throw tantrums, but this is a way of God saying you still have a bit more of spiritual growing to do in order to sustain the blessings coming your way.

I remember throwing hissy fits, but they never made God move any faster. Pity parties will not bring your blessings any quicker. I'm pretty sure every time we conduct ourselves this way, God is probably saying, "Let me know when you are done with your childish ways." I couldn't understand why in the world God had me so long in this dry and silent season, and it wasn't until I surrendered to "what is," that things started to shift for good. When we refuse to accept where God has us, the journey will seem longer and your heart will be in great distress. There are many hidden blessings in your present moment, but you will miss out on the bigger picture as long as you are dwelling on what you don't have. Why would you allow yourself to continue living this way?

Life is way too short to be sitting around thinking about what went wrong, what's going wrong, and what will go wrong. This type of attitude will lead you into a straight depression, cause you to feel like there's no purpose in your life, and steal precious years from you. Let's be real, this happens to many women, especially when we perceive the waiting to be longer than we predicted. What a slap to God's face. We think we will find pure joy in a man (which will never happen), instead of in the Creator who has already given us unconditional love. We are seeking love in all the wrong places.

Men will let us down, even when we are married. We can't put that type of responsibility on another human being. A man is not responsible for your happiness or the love you are seeking. Once you get to a place of honesty where you can genuinely love and trust God, you will feel this internally, which will exude externally—a woman who knows her value doesn't come across as needy. There's nothing more attractive than a woman who is completed by the love of God.

If we look at our path like the alphabet, we won't grow weary. To get to Z, you have to go through all the letters in the alphabet. There's a valuable lesson in every letter. It's the same concept as when we are going after our dreams; we have to go through different seasons and there will be uncomfortable moments, but to get to the end goal you have to put your seatbelt on and enjoy the many bumpy rides. All sorts of monkey wrenches will be thrown your way; you don't know when or what they will be. If you let go of how you want your life to unfold, it will be a smoother ride.

Here's the thing: when you know God has your back and He wants nothing but the very best for you, you can release your anxieties. Follow your instincts at all times. It is only when you go against your intuition that you will you be dishonoring your inner truth. Jeremiah 29:11 says, "'For I know the plans I have for you,' declares the Lord, 'plans to prosper you and not to harm you, plans to give you hope and a future.'" You shouldn't want anyone or anything He hasn't ordained for you.

I understand everything that comes our way is not always from God. You have to be able to decipher what is of God and what is a distraction. This could be tricky, especially if you are a person who likes to overthink everything. Prayer without forcing something to happen is the best way to judge which one is which. When I feel something heavy in my spirit, I know for sure it is a diversion. The conflict comes when I ignore what I feel is wrong. This is when we put ourselves in relationships we don't belong in.

Don't open doors God has shut; this should be a clear sign for you to continue pushing through. God will open doors you are meant to walk through, allowing you to walk a clear path without any stumbling. Let Him be the pilot of your life. When you allow Him to be a pilot, you will have a sense of peace with no confusion, no matter how hard the task at hand is. He will give you the strength, and you may not even understand how you got through the toughest seasons of your life. Listen to the inner voice that is consistently guiding you.

There will be certain frogs coming your way, but it doesn't mean you have to kiss them all to find out which is your prince. When you have a clear mind and don't allow your fear to run your life, you will be able to smell the funk from a mile away and throw the frog right back to where it came from.

This takes me back to what we were talking about; as soon as you sense something is not right with a man you are dating or just met, you have to be willing to let him go. Don't try to conform to his ways so that you won't be single. It's not ever going to work, and

I'm talking from experience. I've done both ... I've done the letting go and holding on, only to later find out he wasn't the man God had in store for me. It shouldn't take you months to figure out if the guy is from God or not. You will know right away. Just as fast as you get the feeling of "something is not right," you will also get the feeling of "this feels right."

This is why you shouldn't tell all your friends about everyone you meet. Some guys are not even worth talking about, it's a waste of energy. You may even feel like a loser if you find yourself telling your friends over and over again, "It didn't work out." The worse feeling is when people may think something is wrong with you. You keep your mouth shut until you receive confirmation from the Lord. Plus, it would sway your decision if you have to cut him off. It's tougher when your friends think he's cute and now you feel like you won't find someone better. Nope, girl, don't fall for the delusional concept of wanting to prove to anyone you have a man in your life.

Save that time for the one God has created just for you. Don't go spreading your love to everyone, and by the time the one comes, you won't even know how to love. When you go giving your heart to people who don't deserve it, you will soon start building a shield, a wall of protection. The wall will create fear, bitterness, resentment, and anxiety. You will give up on true love because you were too busy entertaining fools who weren't even supposed to be in your space, but you let them in due to your insecurity about being alone.

Let's talk about killing time with someone until the "one" arrives. Yes, I'm going to call it what it is. You can't play these types of games with God. What is exactly killing time anyways? You could be devoting this time to God and learning as much as you could about yourself. Keeping it one hundred, "killing time," will only diminish your spirit. Be brave and courageous and know there's no wasted time when you spend it in the right area. Lending your heart and time to people who are not your ideal mate will only keep you further from meeting the one God has for you.

You do have a choice. You have to make up your mind; you will not spend a single moment with a man who is not God-sent. I said this before; you don't need to go kissing many frogs to find out who's your prince. Life is way too short and precious to go wasting it with just anyone. Remember, it's all about growth and trusting that God will answer when He knows you are ready.

Thank everyone in the past who walked away. Little do you know now, but you will soon know how much of a favor it was. It was God saying, "Daughter, this is not your door." Don't try to figure out why the door didn't open or why it only cracked open. God will reveal to you these things when He deems it necessary. There is a reason why I talk about being very sure about who you are in Christ. Some people may read it as arrogance, but a woman with purpose and who trusts in the Lord will be seen as a God-fearing woman who attracts nothing but abundance. When you have a clear vision about the direction you are heading in, the "killing time" goes out the window.

You are so comfortable in your skin that your alone time is not lonely time, but loving time. You won't let any average Joe come into your life. You will be selective and take your time to see if the person is even worthy of a conversation with you. Trust me, this type of confidence is exuded externally, and men will know from a mile away that they can't run game on you. When you have come to a place of loving yourself fully, the right one will approach you the right way. There will be no games or selfish motives.

Men can also smell needy women, so please don't be that girl. If you are the only one taking all the initiative for when to meet up, making phone calls, sending text messages, or making dinner plans, you have been identified as "needy." God never intended for women to go after men. Hint: there is a reason God created Adam before Eve, and Eve came from Adam's rib. II Timothy 2:13 says, "For Adam was formed first, and then Eve." You don't need to chase or force a man to spend time with you or call you. If he doesn't do it, he's not that into you; accept it and keep it moving. You can thank him now that you know he's not the one.

I had a tough time being submissive to God. The word alone made me quiver. I would make demands that now make me laugh. I wanted things my way, plus I didn't think there was anything wrong with asking a guy to meet until I (painfully) learned that this is not God's way. Luckily, I discovered quickly how men think. We are two different species; they don't think like us and vice versa. We make them a lot more complicated than they are. It's probably our overthinking habits that make us think men are convoluted creatures.

We vindicate their actions when really, they're black or white. Men don't have a whole lot of gray, as we do. They may communicate indirectly, but read between the lines and look at their actions. It's hilarious to hear back some of the conversations my friends and I would have about the men we were talking to at the time. The men seemed emotionally unavailable, but we know now they just didn't see us as the one. We wanted to justify their actions to make us feel better about why we were keeping them around.

Some of the excuses we heard were: I'm focusing on my career; I have to deal with my childhood issues; what's the rush, let's give it some time to get to know each other; I love you and need some time, but trust that I will commit. Have you heard any of these, even a few? It's a way of a guy telling you that you are not the one. He doesn't see a future with you. Don't wait around thinking you can get him to change his mind. Get out of it now! Men were created to hunt and conquer. I know you are trying to ease your hurt from rejection, but accept it, he's not trying to win you.

I've never seen women who chase men work for the long haul. Men were designed to be hunters, and by being a woman who's doing the chasing, you are taking away what God formed the man to be and do. I know is even harder for women in leadership positions. We are used to making decisions and making things happen; it's an automatic default when it comes to our love lives. It won't work in this area of our lives, and you have to let the man be the man. Yes, this means being submissive and allowing him to take charge.

I always thought it was pathetic, but when I started reading the word of God and listening to my true essence, I learned that our husbands should be the ones taking the lead. We are taking away their masculinity when we undercut their normal masculine instincts. From the beginning of time, men always were on a hunt. Their natural tendency is to provide and protect. Ladies, don't cringe, it's liberating to know we weren't made to do it all. I know I'm usually exhausted after a long day at work, after having to lead and manage people. It's invigorating to come home and not have to make all the rulings.

A man who's genuinely after God's heart will hear God's voice telling him how to proceed. He will take the necessary actions to show you he wants you in his life. He will shower you in ways you couldn't even imagine. Don't fool yourself into thinking that if you can get him spending more time with you, he will deepen his feelings. He may take up your offer at times, but this is just empty companionship. The guy will ultimately end whatever you guys have going on. It is in his nature to hunt, and you have taken away his primary purpose. Don't be the crazy girl trying to lock in a man! You don't need to manipulate the situation; if you do, he will run faster than Forrest Gump. Be the lady you were created to be, a flower letting nature take its course.

We tend to think that every man we meet may be the one. If you have this sort of mindset, it will cloud your judgment. You won't be able to see the person for who they are or, even worse, you will justify his actions. It's imperative to be level-minded and ready to let go if you feel your gut telling you he's not the one. You won't be able to hear the soft whispers in your heart if you are trying to predict your future. You don't know how your life is going to unfold.

If you are currently in this predicament, don't ignore the soft voice telling you what you need. The longer you wait to follow what your intuition is telling you to do, the longer you are taking to receive your manifestation.

Don't be as stubborn as I was, or as fearful I was at one time. Whatever it is you feel you should be doing, go all in. Don't wait for the perfect timing, because there is no perfect timing. The time is now, let go of everything that's not serving your highest good!

Remember what I've kept telling you: loneliness is a terrible place to be. But I do know the hardest decisions are usually the best ones. You have to ask yourself what you want and stick to it no matter what temptation or adversity comes your way. You may be feeling like you've been on this trail too long and need a man, any man. You can't allow your emotions to lead you. Being influenced by dysfunctional feelings will prohibit you from entering into the next chapter of your life. Face your fears and make a declaration that you will do what God is asking you to do.

Pain stems from reminiscing about your past or thinking about your future and when you stay present, the fear will start fizzing away. God is with you through the whole process. It's okay to allow yourself to feel the pain, but then let it go. Don't run into another dangerous situation because you are afraid of being by yourself. Tell yourself, "I have made a promise to God and myself that I will not compromise.

The God who has given me so many blessings over my life will be the same God who will bring forth the husband He has ordained for me, in His perfect timing." Keep repeating it until your heart starts to believe it. Let me emphasize the importance of staying away from any social media or reality shows when you are going through this transformation.

Exposing yourself to distractions will only hinder your walk and strength; they will not empower you. They are nothing but pure distractions leading you farther from your true essence. Take this time to create a vision board; it will keep your focus on what you are praying for and believing. Cut out and paste on a poster board all of the desires you want to bring forth this year. Put it in a place where you can meditate on it day and night until it becomes rooted into your subconscious. Once you get to a place of feeling like you've already received the life you are looking for is when you will start attracting it to you.

When a man approaches you who is below your standards, you will be okay saying, "Sorry, I'm not interested." You will have an obvious vision of what you want and deserve. To make it clear, I'm not talking about the physical but the internal—you will have a clear view of the values you are seeking in a man. When you don't have a target you are aiming for, you will start aiming everywhere, which means you will begin to allow any man into your space or be afraid to let the old ones go.

Step into this new chapter with full confidence that God is going to do immeasurably more than you can even imagine. Having the vision board gives you a boost of confidence needed to know it's all coming in its perfect divine order and timing; no need to stress about it.

At the beginning of every January, I rallied my team to work on a vision board. I had one employee in particular who once shared hers with me. One of her pictures was a brown leather couch she wanted for her living room. A few months later, miraculously, an on-air jock was moving and had a brown leather couch she needed to give away. She called my employee to see if she wanted it, and, of course, she was in awe to see how this had manifested. She also put the desired income she needed to achieve that year on her board. And guess what? She earned what she put on there. Her job is not salaried, it's one hundred percent commission.

I was so excited for her! I've also had many experiences like these. They don't always happen within the year we envision, but they do manifest themselves if you do the necessary work to achieve them. My boards never have Gucci bags or Louboutin shoes, but things and experiences that are going to help me grow. Don't get me wrong, if that's what you are seeking, by all means, add that to your vision board, but also add items that are going to lead you to become a better you. You can add the following: traveling (expands your mind), purchasing a house (equity), going back to school (enhances your career path), marriage and kids (love), building a stronger relationship with God (unconditional love and peace). It's great to have pictures or sayings that are going to push you to your purpose. Set aside a few minutes to go deep within yourself to uncover what you would like to create in your universe in the next twelve months.

Here's another example of what happens when your board is full of superficiality. I had another employee who was going through a lot of drama related to men in her life. I would give her advice, but for whatever reason, she kept going in the wrong direction. Well, it turned out all the images on her vision board had to do with travel and material things.

Don't get me wrong, there's nothing shady about material objects, but the foundation wasn't there. She was seeking men to buy her the items and take her to remarkable places. This explained why she had so much drama with men; she was attracting the wrong type of men. She wasn't looking for love; she was seeking a sugar daddy. Subconsciously, she was creating a disastrous life. She didn't stay long with our company.

Does this surprise you? She was bringing all this bad luck unto herself. This is why it's so critical to listen to the still voice. Find out what your real purpose is and create a plan for how you are going to achieve it. The vision board will provide insights into your psyche, which is excellent. It will allow you to make the necessary changes to be able to draw in what you've put on the board.

When you start meditating on your board, at first it will feel like nothing is happening. The dreams or desires seem far-fetched, and to top it off every time you get a glimpse of your visions manifesting, you are let down. It feels even worse when everyone around seems to be living their dreams while you are waiting on the sideline, questioning if you are cursed. It does sound a bit dramatic, right? But the truth is, this is what we do when we allow our minds to play tricks on us. How do you make it past your thoughts? The reality is, everything you are feeling is based on how you perceive your life. You can meet someone who's going through a hard time but has a positive outlook on the situation and believes it's all going to work out.

Figure out what the lesson is so you can quickly get out of the rut. As soon as you yield to what is, instead of what should be, you will feel free and joyful. Now, it's not something you do once and think it's going to change everything. It's continually training your brain so that you won't let it dwell in your pain. You have to prime the mind to think positive.

Are you wondering how to do this when we seem like we are always thinking the worst scenario? For starters, you have to stay away from negative people, TV shows, and places that are going to diminish your power. This is not new information, and I'm pretty sure you've heard it in many various ways. Have you ever listened to a song and ten minutes later you are still singing it? It's because what we feed our minds regularly with will resonate within our subconscious. Invest yourself in positive books, motivational videos, and environments that will lift your spirit up.

Friends and family can be a delicate balance, since some can consume your energy, but when you find your strength being sucked out, even with people at work, detach yourself. You don't have to say anything, just politely remove yourself from the location. Be attentive with someone who needs advice versus someone who wants to gossip or be negative. Don't participate in the party. Sometimes, we add more to our troubles by allowing people's problems to become ours. What we absorb is also what we expose; garbage in, garbage out. When your plans are not unfolding the way you thought they would, or your prayers are going unanswered, remind yourself God sits high and looks low. He knows exactly what you are going through, but He's not troubled by your clock. He knows when to answer your prayers. If you are indeed putting your best foot forward, God is handling all of your affairs.

Try your hardest not to make anything happen before its proper timing. When you try to rush God's timing, you get yourself into circumstances that either you are not mentally mature enough to handle and sabotage them, or it was never your door to go through. When we want something so obsessively, we start pursuing things that were never meant to be part of our plan. Eventually, it doesn't work out and you are back to square one, but now with pain and sorrow in your heart.

I've done it a few times in my life. I'm often reminded of the repercussions that occurred when I went against my spirit and followed my flesh. Maybe it worked out for you, which I doubt, but it didn't work out for me.

We have to be powerful women and need to finish strong. Yes, you will experience loneliness, betrayal, and disappointments, but they're all part of the task of getting to your desires. It will feel overwhelming at times, especially when you think things are getting worse, but you have to continue moving forward no matter what. God wouldn't have brought you this far only to stop you in your tracks. When God knows it's the right time to manifest your desires, He will come in and show out. He will make sure you know that there was no way you could've done it on your own. Understand there is a purpose and a reason for everything. Ladies, stay firm and courageous and don't give up. I don't care what it looks like or feels like; you have to be bigger than the situation.

CHAPTER SIX

USE YOUR PAIN TO PUSH YOU TOWARD YOUR TARGET

Let the heartbreaks you've gone through lead you to your life's purpose. This chapter is about identifying who you are and what excites you. Don't wait for your husband to arrive before you find your calling, or even worse, conform to what you think your husband wants you to be. Ladies, deep inside there's something you've been called to do that no one else in this universe can do quite like you.

Here's a thought: if, God forbid, you committed a crime and fled the country, they would find you. You know why? Fingerprints. No human being on this entire planet has the same fingerprints as yours—doesn't that make you think? It means God designed you for a specific purpose. Isn't it intriguing to see God's work? It's so mysterious, yet so fascinating, to know the Lord made you intentionally. He has a game plan He needs to accomplish through you. Together, let's discuss what your God-given purpose is.

Take a few minutes to close your eyes to meditate on what exhilarates you. This sensation makes you feel all types of butterflies in your stomach. When you are operating on what excites you and you lose track of time, this is called your "PURPOSE." This is one of the main reasons why God created you. Are you doing it full time? If not, why not? Are you afraid to take a leap of faith? Don't be scared to go after what you know is right in your heart. There's a risk in everything we do, so why not take a chance to go after your dream instead of working a job that literally makes you sick? When you wake up every day without following your purpose, you are doing a disservice to yourself and the people who need your service.

I've always had an acute awareness that I was called to be a transformational coach, but it wasn't until my ex walked away and I continued through my journey that my calling became absolutely clear. Sometimes heartbreak brings us to our purpose in our lives. You have to know painful flashes happen in your life to birth something inside of you. I have other interests I find myself intrigued by, such as dancing, working out, sales, and marketing. All of these excite me, but the area I find myself most fulfilled by is encouraging others. I am filled with joy and gratitude when I see a person's light bulb turn on. You may be great at helping the youth, working out, professionally dancing, leading a team, cooking, home decoration, banking; the list is endless. Whatever you are passionate about, go all in. Take this time to work on your purpose instead of trying to figure out when your husband is going to show up.

Journal your thoughts every day to track your progress. Be aware of your daily activities to verify whether they're pushing you towards your goals. It would be deleterious if you missed this part of your life. There's never the perfect timing to start doing what you love; in fact, something will come up to keep you from living the life you are supposed to. Excuses only sound useful to those making them. Make it a point this week to write down what you want to achieve in the next five days.

It's an attractive trait when you know exactly where you are going. You don't need to know all the moving parts, but you do need to see the end goal. You will look much more attractive and confident to the people around you. You will exude this beauty that only comes from knowing who you are in Christ and being complete. When God created you, He had a purpose in mind—He doesn't produce anything unless there's a master plan behind it. Ask God for His master plan concerning you and He will reveal it.

It doesn't matter if it seems too immense, you have to make a leap of faith. He will give you the abilities you need to accomplish each step. It will take a lot of faith and courage when you encounter hurdles, but knowing your end goal will keep you going. I've had my share of barriers; some were easy to jump over and some took everything in me.

What I've learned is that each obstacle has a lesson, but what happens with many women is they get stuck on how hard it is and never find out what they are capable of becoming and consummating. Life will throw some huge rocks at you, but the great news is that you have been designed to break them all. You serve an Almighty Sovereign Lord who's already equipped you with everything you need to get through the barriers. Can you look at life and say, "You will not stop me, I will become everything I came to this earth to be"?

There's something very sexy about a woman who has her life together before a man comes into her world. Ask any man who has good intentions and has an intimate relationship with God. He will tell you that a woman who's chasing after her own life's goals is much more attractive than a woman who's waiting for a man to save her. Be purposeful in life! You only have one shot on Earth, make it count.

It's significant to know who you are before you enter a relationship. You must know what your core values are. For example, if God is essential to you, it will be hard, almost impossible, to have a relationship with someone who doesn't see a relationship with God as one of his core values. Be aware of the man who says he believes in God but his actions show you otherwise. Does this man pray with you? Is this man willing to go to church with you? Does this man respect the woman God created you to be? I've found myself with men who claimed to be believers, but their actions were contrary to what they claimed.

If a guy is out with his friends almost every weekend in places only single men are hanging out or he won't step a foot into a church—even if you paid him—more than likely this man is not ready to be in a serious relationship. They always have such an amusing excuse about why they can't make it to church. If a man tells you God knows his heart so he doesn't need to go to church, be keenly suspicious of this man—as a matter of fact, run. You have to realize when you are walking with God one hundred percent, He will hold you accountable for your behavior. Many people shy away from getting closer to God because they refuse to let go of their ways. Don't get it twisted, I know there are men in the church who are rebels, but God eventually reveals them in the light.

One of the primary reasons divorce rates have increased substantially is because people enter the courtship with different core values and try to get the other person to change. The person will only resent you if you go into a union thinking you can change them. You can't shift a person's behavior; it's hard enough trying to adjust yourself. Please don't compromise who you are to try to make a relationship work. Knowing who you are at your core is so imperative.

The first eighteen months of a relationship are all emotions. You are high as a kite, feeling all types of butterflies in your stomach. After these eighteen months, new feelings will settle in, and reality will be there to smack you right on the face. It's important not to make any life-changing decisions until after you've gotten to know this person very well. Are your core values, common interests, and future goals aligned? If you two are opposites, you will start seeing this clearly, but the problem will be that your emotions are so involved now, it's hard to detach yourself. Before putting yourself in this predicament, make sure the person you are dating has the qualities you are looking for in a life partner. Don't let your fears rule you. Life is too precious and short to settle. You have to be acutely aware of the woman you are becoming before letting someone into your world.

You've been through enough heartbreaks to have learned what guys you need to stay away from. Hopefully, you are utilizing these lessons in your life so you will avoid repeating the same craziness. Take all the time you need to get to know yourself. Don't get caught up in what society is saying, or even what your family is murmuring about your biological clock ticking. I know you feel you need to be married by thirty, or maybe you are over thirty and still not married.

Maybe you are assuming your dreams are diminishing—the Cinderella wedding, two kids, white picket fence (all the crap put into the heads of women) look like they are never going to happen. But let me ask you this question: who told you that you would have all of this by a certain age? I haven't found anywhere in the Bible where God gave an age and time we would each be getting married. Who in the world even made these rules up? I guess someone said, "Thirty sounds about right," and everyone started following that trend. Don't get caught up in the nonsense. If you are in your thirties, or even in your forties, please don't get discouraged.

Just like when I started writing this book, I didn't understand its purpose, but as I continued through the journey I could see small glimpses of clarity. I know part of it was to tell you about the miracles I've encountered and the many lessons I learned along the way. It cost me a lot emotionally and physically to let God deal with me. Are you willing to pay the price? Are you ready to go through whatever is needed to become the best version of yourself? There's a price to pay for those who are seeking greatness. There's no other way. Whoever said there would be no pain and there's a shortcut to this thing called "life," was deceiving you, and he or she is not living to their fullest potential. The bigger the challenge, the bigger the blessing.

Always keep this phrase close to your heart when life seems to be going against you: Mark 9:23 says, "Everything is possible for the one who believes." You have to see the goodness in all of the cloudiness. I see God's unconditional love and all the blessings He's poured into my life. Sometimes you have to reflect on how far you've come. The same God who did it before will do it again, and again, and again.

I made a major mistake by trying to pressure my ex of four years into marrying me. And do you want to know why I was urging him to do so? Yes, you guessed right, because society said I needed to be married by my early thirties.

One beautiful day in May, my ex surprised our family, friends, and me with a lovely trip. I ruined the trip for myself by being in my head and my feelings. I just thought he was going to propose because he invited our friends and family. Now where I am in life, I can tell you neither of us knew what marriage meant. I just felt I didn't want to miss out on the train society was riding. I gave this man an ultimatum that if he didn't marry me by September of that year, our relationship would be over. He didn't propose—instead he walked away shortly after, which in hindsight it was a blessing in disguise.

The moment he decided he no longer wanted to continue the relationship was the moment I began my soul-searching. It's interesting how pain can lead to more significant blessings. I've evolved so much as a woman of God and would have completely missed my life's calling if he had accepted my ultimatum. Marriage is more than a feeling. It's vital to be evenly yoked and have God as the center of your relationship. We were both immature, still trying to figure out life. We both came from a single-parent household, which, of course, can create a lot of insecurities, especially if the parent raising you is dysfunctional and dealing with their own hurt and pain. He was in the NBA trying to figure out his career while I had just gotten promoted. It already looked like we were heading down two distinct paths. He left me a two-page letter communicating where he was in life and why he wasn't sure if he loved me enough to marry me.

Hmmm, hello, I realize now that I wasn't sure if I loved him enough to marry him either. The reason I say this is because I didn't fully know who I was. How in the world could I love my husband if I didn't know who I was? You can't genuinely love someone else until you have fallen in love with yourself. You will fall in love with every single thing about you, even all your imperfections that make you perfectly made in God's eyes.

If you are genuinely seeking marriage, it will come to you, but you first have to seek God above all things. Let go of all worries and anxieties about your biological clock. Stop thinking all types of craziness, believing that if you don't achieve this by the time you've decided you are ready you have failed and your life is over. Your life is not over, and this world is still going.

God promised Sarah and Abraham a baby, but it didn't happen right away. Sarah was at an old age when the blessing came to pass. She even doubted God and took matters into her own hands, which you already know created a lot more chaos. How many times have we done this? It never brings us peace. Genesis 21:1 says, "The Lord kept his word and did for Sarah exactly what he had promised." Jesus kept his promise. Even when it seems like He's not ever going to answer your prayers, be of great courage, my friend—God will make sure your deepest desires will come to pass.

Prayer:

Jesus, I release my concerns about receiving a husband and children. You know these are my deepest desires, but I know you already know these things. I ask you to make me whole and lead me on the path you need me on, so when my husband does arrive, I'm fully ready to receive him with a Godly heart.

If you felt the prayer deep in your heart, God will step in, but now you have to do your part. The Bible tells us in James 2:17, "In the same way, faith by itself if it is not accompanied by action, is dead." It's going to take work on your part. It's going to take more work than you anticipate. Remember, your timing is not God's timing, and there will be moments when you will feel like giving up. But whatever you do, don't hand over your power. Trust God, who created the universe and everything in it; He is the same God who knows exactly how to put the pieces of your life back better than before. Do whatever is required of you in this season.

Finding out what excites you deep within your soul is so imperative. You need to start working on it right away, without making excuses about why you can't do it. Read books that are going to elevate you and teach you new things in life. Listen to motivational videos on YouTube. Also, go to a few conferences, if possible, with panelists you admire. Surround yourself with women who are seeking growth in their lives and are doing something about it. Find time to exercise so you can feel good about yourself internally and externally. Just work on you!

Whatever you do, *do not* get with your other bitter girlfriends to chat about how miserable you guys are, and how there are no good men out there. Change your inner circle if needed. Take control of your life. You have to make drastic changes in your inner space to receive the abundant life you are expecting God to bring forth. You can't be negative and expect positive results. Self-awareness is imperative in this season of your life. Listen to yourself talk. Do you speak life or death? Proverbs 18:21 says, "The tongue has the power of life and death, and those who love it will eat its fruit."

Be careful with what you are saying and make sure what you articulate is not contradicting what you are asking for from God. God pays attention to our hearts; you can quickly tell a person's heart based on their actions. If you are expressing words or behaving in a way that is not of God, you need to transform immediately. There's no need to call your friends or family for some intervention—discuss it with God and then sit in silence to hear His instructions. He will reveal the areas where you need to begin making adjustments. Some of the girlfriends you are surrounding yourself with are not elevating you to your highest good. You need people who are going to help you grow, to propel you to become the very best version of yourself.

I'm swift to detach myself from people who don't exemplify the direction I'm on or heading. I don't judge them, as they are entitled to live their lives the ways they wish to, but I know what I want and where I want to go. Even if this means being by myself momentarily until God brings me a new group of women, I will do it. Growth is too significant to me, and I understand that if I hang with someone long enough, their ways will become mine.

Do you have friends you need to break off from? Also, be open-minded about your new circle. You have no idea who God will be sending your way. Remember, you are going through a cleansing which means the toxic old habits and behaviors will be gradually diminishing. The people who you used to attract into your life will no longer be drawn to you. You will be mingling with folks who were never on your radar. These people are a reflection of what's in your heart and the direction God is taking you. The places you hung out at will no longer give you peace. You will find yourself uninterested, and your facial expressions will be priceless when observing the foolishness you were unaware of before. You will think to yourself, why were you ever attracted to these places? When God goes to work, your heart will be completely altered and your mind renewed. It's all part of the expanding season. You won't be interested in the men you mingled with in the past. Your taste will entirely shift, and you won't even know when or how it happened.

I remember the day I was hit with the things I'd been asking God to reveal and change started to manifest. My inner circle, hangout spots, conversations, perspective in life, and taste in men . . . they all transformed. I was a new woman and adoring who I was becoming. I had a lot more like-minded people around me, people who wanted to do something more with their lives. They had big dreams and saw life from a different lens. I discerned that my life was finally going in a purposeful direction. My actions finally aligned with who I was at my core.

People may judge you for the moves you are making. Don't get caught up with their opinions; keep transforming. Family members are sometimes the first ones to talk nonsense about the new you. They may even feel like you think you are better than them, but who cares what they are saying? What matters the most is that you show them the results. Once they see the positive effects in your life, some will start following your lead. Don't be intimidated to take big jumps. It will require letting go of an old boo, job, friends, and even family.

Even in the beginning of times, God was always asking us to do what would be uncomfortable and, at times, scary. God told Abraham in Genesis 12:1, "Leave your native country, your relatives, and your father's family, and go to the land that I will show you." As you all know, Abraham went on to accomplish many great things, but it doesn't mean he didn't endure many hardships. He faced many giants as he was going toward what God had promised him, but he never gave up on God or lost his faith.

Thank You for Walking Away would've never been birthed if I didn't jump. All the pain I experienced brought me to the very moment of knowing who I was becoming and my life's mission. Oh, how I thank my exes, friends, family, and even jobs that walked away from me. Thank you for shutting the door right smack in my face. I now understand those weren't my doors, and it was God's protection saving me for His very best plans. He has an original plan for me with doors specifically with my name on them. No one will be able to walk through those doors but me. Let the grief build a stronger you, and those muscles will help you sustain peace when life decides to throw another curve ball your way.

I've emerged in so many areas of my life and have never been so sure of who I am in the way I am now. I've seen a lot in my life and have experienced a lot more than the typical woman in her mid-thirties. God has orchestrated in you and in me to be all He's called us to be. Let's not waste our unique talents. What a shame it would be if God couldn't rely on you to do what He's brought you into this world to do. God will get the job done. The question is if you are going to let Him do the work through you. I hope the answer is yes. If so, let's do this!

I know, it's so much easier said than done, but there's truth in hardships that help us grow. Think about it—if you were sincerely present and honest with yourself, you would agree with me that many of your challenging seasons made you seek God more and allowed you to become a better person. For whatever peculiar reason, in our weakest and darkest moments we seek answers deep within to help us through the tough times.

We need to master how to embrace trials. When God allows battles to come your way, it's because He also knows He will complete them for you. You can handle it! Don't grow weary and quit in the middle of the racket. Hold on to your faith and watch God compensate you for your devotion. I don't know how long it will take you to cross the finish line, but what I do know is His timing is perfect. Just to set the expectations now, let me be bluntly candid with you. It will not be easy. The most significant awards usually come with the most troublesome obstacles. Are you going to want to retreat? Yes. All winners at one point or another felt like resigning, but they didn't give in to their desire to quit. They shook it off and kept it moving.

Take a minute to ponder on the last big issue you had in your life. Did it last forever? Your response more than likely is no because everything does pass. You have to toughen up and tell yourself numerous times throughout the day, "This, too, shall pass" and figure out the lesson for this season. What have you learned that can help you for the next section of your life?

What are some behaviors you must stop? Trust the inner voice and the convictions you feel; they're trying to get your attention before your demeanor leads to more destruction. Life has shown me that the longer I overlook my gut instincts, the longer I will remain in pain. As you proceed to grow in Christ, you will learn to trust the soft inner voice. Like Steve Harvey says, "Jump, you have to jump!" You can't go through life afraid to take chances or refusing to make decisions you know will improve your existence and bring you closer to your goals. JUMP! JUMP! JUMP! He also says the parachute won't open right away, and that's okay. What's most important is that you take one step, and God will make the other one for you.

The most critical part of the journey is learning how to take command of your thoughts. I didn't recognize how suddenly you can change your feelings when they wander off to the negative.

I always questioned how many people were watching me as I was going through a heartbreak and then a tumor to see how I would weather the storm. It is much easier to praise God when everything is going well, but what about when your life seems like you are in hell? Trust me when I tell you people are observing. Are you going to crack? They may even murmur, "Where is your God now?" Unfortunately, many people break and won't see God's fullness manifest in their lives. Be strong-minded to fight the good fight of faith. Ask yourself, "Am I stronger than life?" You are either powerful or weak. You have a choice. Which one are you? When you make sacrifices for a better tomorrow, which means changing your inner circle, reading empowering books, and participating in seminars to help you grow, you are becoming a more powerful and fabulous you.

You have infinite power within you because Christ lives in you. Every season has a termination date, but it's up to you to decide how you are going to react in the middle of the rain. I don't even advise that you date until you have worked on yourself. All the self-doubts will persist if you don't know who you are. When you are living in despair, all your future projections will be like a horror movie. You see your future based on your current situation, and it's the most dangerous thing you can do to your mind, body, and soul. You have to approach dating with full confidence so that you won't attract the wrong energies.

The spirit will radiate so brightly from you because you have done the mandatory work, and you know who you are, your purpose, and the core values you are seeking in a mate. There's nothing sexier than a woman or man who is self-assured. And I'm not saying a person who is flashy, but a person who has this undeniable presence about them. They won't allow anything that clashes with their values and morals to be in their space.

As we all know, we all have so-called "bad days," but we will learn how to stay in the negative space for no longer than one day. Allow yourself to suffer whatever you are feeling and then let it go. When something unpleasant comes up, I don't react right away. I allow myself to breathe and disconnect from the dilemma for a few moments. I ask God how I should handle it, and if I don't hear or sense anything, I put it aside and stand still. Your job is to lean on God and let Him show you the way. But don't be too hard on yourself if the choice you made based on what you thought was right made matters worse. Mistakes are needed to know what not to do again. What matters is that you took action and now you know what not to do.

It wasn't until I started to write down the attributes I was looking for in a husband that it became clear to me what I wanted. It also was an "aha" moment; I hadn't been particular in the past with the men I allowed into my space. When I thought of some of the men I had dealt with, I wanted to kick myself. How did I even let myself go there with some of these fools?

I'll tell you how. I didn't have Christ in the center of my life and wasn't sure who I was. I neglected to put a whole lot of thought into it. All I knew was the guy had to be successful and cute. How vague is that? How far was the external list going to get me? After noticing my disruptive pattern, it became even more imperative to recite the qualities to myself every day and night until I ingrained them into my subconscious. And since the end goal was to have the husband God ordained, I also added scripture to give myself peace with God's plan. Proverbs 19:21 says, "Many are the plans in a person's heart, but it is the Lord's purpose that prevails."

I ultimately wanted the husband God wanted for me. I asked Him to teach me how to discern his voice so that I could follow Him. Always examine your goals with Him and stay quiet to see what your spirit is telling you; He will reveal to you the way. Don't pursue anything or anyone He removes. Keep pushing through no matter what! You won't always detect an answer right away, but you will get your response in God's perfect timing and order.

When we keep a man who's not good for us, it stems from being afraid of singleness. I, too, have done this, but it only hinders you from receiving the one God has for you. Keeping the fool around will bring more pain. You have to make a conscious decision and stand by it to let go of anyone who doesn't serve you to your highest purpose. But let me tell you the number of distractions that will occur when your mind is made up.

I remember the week after saying to myself, "I'm letting go of him—no more foolishness. I will no longer keep a man who I know deep in my heart is not the one." A few days after saying that, men started coming out of the woodwork. I met a successful and good-looking man at my doctor's appointment, and shortly after, another guy I saw at my gym contacted me via LinkedIn. You all know I started thinking God was answering my prayers and it was raining men (I laugh at this now). Of course, random acts will occur. We have to be aware that when we make a commitment to God in a specific area of our lives, the enemy will start attacking us.

What I didn't know was all these men were distractions trying to throw me off of my path. The guy from the gym who just so happened to live in the same condo building as me relocated to the west coast, so I found it quite interesting that he was reaching out ... why would we start talking now when we didn't exchange words while living in the same area? You would have thought it was a visible sign that he wasn't the one, but I fell for it.

Luckily, at this point in my life, I was able to decipher a lot faster if the guy I became involved with felt right or not. I cut him off after a month, and I also let go of the other guy. Again, ladies, you can't be sleeping around with a guy you just met. Imagine if I would have fallen for their games and slept with them. It benefits you not to give up the cookie. If I would've slept with any of the guys I had just met, my vision would have become clouded. When you can see things from a non-sexual interpretation, you will make wiser, life-changing choices.

I was able to see these relationships from God's perspective when there was no carnal attachment. Unless he tells you that you two are in a committed relationship, don't sleep with him. Alternatively, challenge yourself not to have any sexual intercourse until marriage. I don't know, ladies, but doesn't it get tiring when you are continually dealing with the same foolishness? You can't be lending out your heart to men who don't even know how to handle love.

Little by little you will damage who you are by sleeping with men who aren't your soulmate. For many years I fought against the premarital stance. I would tell people, "Show me in the Bible that it's a sin to have sex before marriage." No one was able to show me, but one day as I was reading Acts and Romans, I witnessed with my own eyes how premarital sex was forbidden. I was dumbfounded and couldn't avoid the conviction in my soul as I was reading the scriptures.

I reflected on the men I had given my body to and where it all had led me so far. I understood why the Lord was advising us to avoid sex before marriage. I realized that when the intimacy happened, I lost

ANGELINA ROSARIO

my power. Being emotionally intertwined with the person will make it much harder to let go. Being blinded by the sex will only cloud your judgment on him. We will ignore the guy's disorderly behavior and the pain he is causing you.

A lack of information will keep us in bondage, suffering from all types of irrational problems. God comprehends the significance of two people making love. He's the one who created sex, but when we go against His will by engaging in pre-marital relations, sex can become more hurtful than good. I get it, there's a vast number of marriages that didn't practice celibacy, but let's also look at the increase in the divorce rate. I bet it was all the great sex that influenced their decision to get married.

Do you know the role dopamine plays in decision-making? Dopamine is one of the chemical signals that passes information from one neuron to the next in the tiny spaces between them. In layman's terms, it causes addiction. Sex can become an addiction, just like a drug addict is always looking for the next high. When we allow sex to rule us, we will continuously confuse lust with genuine love. The main reason the average marriage lasts for about five years is because they get married while they are high on dopamine, only to find out a few years later they have nothing in common. This became evident to me, and I was ready to take a leap of faith with God regarding celibacy.

When you give every area of your life to God, new miracles will materialize. God does give us free will; He will not force Himself on you. You will have to be willingly and openly receptive to His will. I don't believe He will stop blessing you entirely, but you will not get the fullness He has in store for you. Let's say that when you live outside of His plan, even your best will be mediocrity in His world. Every day we are shaping our world with our actions.

Our decisions shape every second of our day. Situations will pop up as we are going through what I call our journey, and you may have no control over them. What you can do is learn from whatever they are trying to teach you, and ask God to help you get through them better and stronger. Les Brown, a great motivational speaker, said one of the most life-changing actions you can do to get your day started right is to listen or do something positive as soon as you wake up for twenty minutes. Your first twenty minutes after awakening will determine how the rest of your day will unfold. This ritual has refined my life utterly. When unexpected problems arise during the day, I handle them without being erratic. On the contrary, if I play hooky, my day is not as productive. My mind tends to wander off, and I sort of just become stagnant, or what I like to call a walking zombie.

How do we expect to be our best and be a blessing to another if the first thing we do when we awaken is to check our phones? The reality is, many people start their day by monitoring social media, news, and emails. When you fill your thoughts with negative junk, it will be a domino effect for the rest of your day. Make sure you are fueling your mind every morning with prayer, meditation, affirmations, visualizations, and gratitude to train our mind to think optimistically. Of course, you will have down moments, but you will find yourself snapping out of them much quicker.

CHAPTER SEVEN

PRAYER AND MEDITATION

I discovered prayer and meditation are the only two formulas that rejuvenate your heart, mind, and spirit. I'm not sure if you are one to believe in prayers, but I'm here to tell you they work. I don't know where I would be if I didn't have a direct relationship with our Heavenly Father. When I learned that prayer is nothing more than a conversation with God, it changed my life entirely.

I used to think prayer had to be long-winded and I had to know the Bible from start to finish. I always keep it one hundred with God. I go before Him with an open heart, telling Him exactly how I feel. He already knows what you are feeling and thinking, so why not be sincere? He wants to hear you and help you; He wants to build an intimate relationship with you. When you come to Him with an unobstructed heart, He will step in and do what you can't do.

My first encounter with prayer was when I was eight years old. I was home alone and couldn't find the keys to the front door anywhere in the house. My mom was extremely stern when it came to making sure we always had the keys handy, since back in those days the front door could only be opened and closed with the key. Being petrified my mother would lay hands on me for losing them, I went into my mom's room where she had a Virgin Mary sculpture on top of her dresser. I got down on my knees and cried out loud to her, "Please help me find the key." I kid you not, minutes later I heard keys falling on the ground from the other room. I opened my eyes, slowly got up from my knees, and started walking nervously to the separate bedroom while my heart was racing. Lo and behold, the keys were on the floor! As an eight-year-old, I thought there was a ghost in our home. I panicked, jetted to the front door, and hung out outside until my mother came from work. Thinking back to this day still brings warmth to my heart, to see the power of prayer at such a young age.

Why is it many of us only seek God when are facing trials and tribulations? This makes me think God also knew we would only learn and grow when faced with such circumstances. I remember when I was living life on my terms, without once consulting on any of it with God, I was led onto an agonizing path. It took a while for me to grasp why praying to God daily would direct me to my purpose. Maybe I was permitting religion to deter me from having a faithful relationship with Him. I felt I needed to be a perfect woman for God to accept me into His family. It was even more complicated when working in the entertainment business, especially when you are told it's the devil's playground.

I was conflicted with my life's calling versus what religious people were preaching. I would get overwhelmed with all the rules about prayer; I would say, "The heck with all of this." It wasn't until I turned inward and surrendered it all to God, without worrying about being judged, when praying became the most valuable time of my day. Working in the entertainment business where there's plenty of corruption with sex, drugs, and alcohol made it even more challenging to think God loved me. But soon I would learn that there are plenty of people in showbiz who are God-fearing and living righteously. It wasn't until I devoted time to prayer that I was able to release the misconceptions of what prayers should sound like, who I needed to be, or the length of time I should be praying.

One day in my early twenties, I decided to have an in-depth conversation with God. I kept it one hundred. I didn't recite scriptures or embellish anything; I just kept it authentic. I told Him I'd lost my way in life and I didn't know my purpose anymore. I needed Him to help me find my way. After my prayer, I felt so much lighter, like the heaviness I was carrying all of a sudden came off of me. God doesn't want us going to Him pretending to be someone we are not. He already knows who we are, so in the end we are only deceiving ourselves. Every time I have a conversation with God about my concerns or worries, He always gives me peace. He doesn't necessarily solve the issue right away, but He gives us peace and strength to deal with whatever the problem or fear is at the time.

Religion has made us feel as though we have fallen short of trying to live a righteous life and that we are not worthy enough of having an intimate relationship with Jesus Christ. This couldn't be further from the truth. God accepts us exactly as we are, no matter where we are. He's ready to receive us the moment we give our lives to Him and surrender it all. God can do so much more with our imperfections. He uses our flaws in ways we can't. People will be left wondering how you achieved what you've accomplished so far. This is why prayer is so indispensable—it is your lifeline.

Prayer is just a conversation with God; it's that simple. I know we've heard people recite fancy prayers, which can be intimidating, but it's just a heart to heart moment with God. Don't let religious folks make you think you can't have a partnership with Him. As I mentioned before, just be yourself and talk to Him just like you would with a best friend. It's not about when He will remove the thorns from your flesh, but giving you the peace and strength to get through the tough moments. Remember, sometimes there are lessons and character-building seasons, and you can't skip this process, but you can have tranquility and sturdiness to deal with it until it passes.

I know people who get angry when it seems like He has taken too long to answer them, but God heard them from the moment they requested His help. Just because He hasn't responded to them the way they feel He should doesn't mean He's not at work. We are His children, and God knows what's best for each one of us. Every level requires a certain amount of mental maturity; if He replied to your prayer too soon, you would sabotage the blessing. Going ahead of Him won't help either, as you will end up in bigger shambles, and even take some steps backward. TD Jakes made the perfect analogy: it's like a ten-year-old child asking for a car versus a sixteen-year-old teen. You wouldn't give a ten-year-old a vehicle because you know they wouldn't even know how to handle it and would lead the child into a dead end. It's the same concept when asking God for something and receiving it before you are mature enough. Growing takes time.

Other times, God knows your request will do you more harm than good, so your specific prayers will not be answered because there's something better in store. This is why spending time with God is so essential. Quieting your mind is how you will find the answers and serenity you are trying to obtain, how you hear the soft voice whispering in your heart. To be able to gain the knowledge and wisdom of meditation will take consistent effort. You will feel awkward and your mind will be racing more than ever the first, second, and even the third time. Kudos to you if you can quiet your mind on the first try, but from my experience and speaking to other friends, meditation takes practice. I suggest starting off with ten minutes a day.

There are several videos of guided meditations on YouTube that will give you a jump start. When I began the practice, it was tough to still my mind; I was thinking more than ever. There were times I would catch myself opening one eye every five seconds to see how much time I had remaining. Yeah, I know, that wasn't meditation, but I refused to quit. When I finally just sat down, took a few deep breaths, and allowed myself to relax, that's when I was able to quiet the mind. After a few months, I found myself having a sense of relief with where I was in life. I wasn't attached to my story any longer.

There are certain situations and people who will no longer be part of your story. You will need to ascertain on how to detach yourself without having any expectations of the outcome. Meditation will help you release yourself from the narrative you have created in your head. When we attach ourselves to our stories, we only chase after temporary fixes. A relationship, money, or a new career will never give us the permanent joy we are trying to achieve. God has blessed me tremendously with a job, money, and a fancy car, and has exposed me to the rich and famous, and can I tell you, none of these things ever brought me real happiness.

I still felt a void, a sadness, no matter how many beautiful items I bought and where I traveled—after a short while, I was empty again. I know the reason He allowed me to experience what I thought I wanted was to show me none of it was going to give me what only He can provide—unconditional love. Of course, He wants you to have a life of abundance, but it is not where you will find your true delight. Release it all to God, and He will support you by giving you the tools and resources needed to get through each chapter. I know it's easier said than done, but the more time you devote to God, the easier it will become. It's like anything else you do repetitively; after a while you become an expert.

Meditation was taking my mind to another magnitude. The practice was allowing me to pay attention to the people in my vicinity and their discussions in a deeper way. For example, do you recall a recent time when you asked someone, "How are you?" and their response was, "Same thing, different day"? It wasn't until I was fully present that I discerned how many people are walking around dejected with no sense of value, which explains why only two percent of the population is wealthy. How can you ever become your best self with this kind of mentality? I even started wondering whether I also responded this way.

For the first time in my life, I was fully in the present, aware of my settings, and dumbfounded by the number of people who fall prey to the victim mindset. It became more obvious among women, so many with bitter hearts, acting like their world collapsed because God had them in a quiet season. I've heard women say, "I'm good being single—I don't need a man." Wow! Now, we all know this is not true; in actuality, a majority of all women want to be married. If you are yearning for it, it's because God wants to provide you with a husband. But if you go around saying silly stuff that you don't even mean deep in your heart, you will block your blessings.

When my friends would say such craziness, I would rebuke it. I knew I'd made my mistakes which led me into many heartbreaks, but I also knew I wasn't giving up on love and wanted marriage and a family—but this time I would do it with God. Meditation and prayer gave me the patience I needed to wait on Him. After a while, once I had given up my novel, I felt it in my heart that God would respond to my prayers. It still amazes me to see how He used my ex walking away to awaken my spirit. I felt the walk was unfamiliar, like nothing I'd experienced before. There's favor behind every pain and tear. It's laborious to see it in the moment, but dark seasons come to help us grow.

I'm sure the women walking around with sour attitudes weren't aware of what they were putting out into the universe. I do know that if they had taken the time to quiet their minds and speak to God about their hurt and pain, they would have a different outlook on life.

I get it, we all go through different types of pain and hurt in our lives, but it's up to you to decide you want to change. We have to be very attentive with the words coming out of our mouths. Your vocabulary will tell you who you are and where you are headed. Proverbs 18:21 tells us, "Death and life are in the power of the tongue, and those who love it will eat its fruits."

When I started encountering the benefits of meditation, I began to apply them to my dating. The stillness enabled clarity. I would go pray and then meditate, asking God, "Lord, is (name of the guy) the husband you have ordained for me?" I stayed still with my eyes closed, took a couple of deep breaths, and remained fully present. When you ask, you will need to detach from any future stories you've created in your mind with this guy, no preconceived notions. If you are not level-minded, you'll be hearing your flesh instead of the truth.

There were moments of perplexity; I couldn't decipher what I was hearing. I would make sure not to make any emotional decisions and allow God to bring me the answer when He was ready to. Remember, God's timing is not our timing, but He does know when to bring your request forth. You may get the answer in a variety of ways. Here are three methods in which God has answered me: a still calm voice whispering into my heart, a sensation in my gut, and God sending me someone or something that gave me the answer.

To master meditation, you have to learn to be fully present, which, of course, as I mentioned, can be fatiguing. So many of us are so used to having our mind control us with future anxieties or past experiences. It wasn't always easy to do what I felt deep within myself the

Holy Spirit was asking me to do. There were a few guys I liked, but I couldn't ignore when I got a confirmation from God that they weren't the one. I have to admit, I would have debates with God because there were a few I was really feeling. But can I tell you, months or even years later, the guys the Lord asked me to let go of didn't match my taste anymore.

Meditation helped me to be cognizant of who I am. It also brought up past issues and pain I've covered up over the years. I understood I was doing the best I knew how at the moment, but I wanted to do better and become who I was designed to be from the moment God originated me. Again, let's thank our exes for walking away. Why would you even want to go into a union with past baggage and garbage? It would be unfair to the person who comes into your life. Plus, I'm pretty sure you would only attract someone who's probably dealing with the same vicious cycles.

Start meditating, even when it feels like you can't quiet your mind at first. We live in a convoluted world where we have family, friends, and co-workers telling us what we should be doing in our lives. I'm sure they mean well, but the majority of them don't have the slightest idea what they are doing with their own lives. Meditation will allow you to detach from their suggestions and you will make resolutions for your specific blueprint.

Another excuse that will keep you from the practice is your so-called busy schedule. I've heard people say they are too occupied to sit in quietness for a minimum of fifteen minutes. You make time for the things you consider essential. If you are wondering why your life feels stagnant, it could be that you are not making the necessary time to get the answers from the source.

In today's world, it's easier for our minds to fill up with junk, and if we are not careful, this will control how we think. When you make decisions based on your emotions, you will find your mind is more cluttered, confused, and going in circles. If you don't see the time to rejuvenate your soul, you will continuously be living in mediocrity. Clear your mind from the disarray, and get a clear vision in what you want.

Alone time with God became so essential that I even built a small sanctuary in a private place in my condo. I have sticky notes with some of my favorite Bible verses, my vision board, spiritual candles, a statue of Jesus Christ, the Virgin Mary, and a few other inspirational items. It's pretty cool, and it keeps my mind focused on love and peace when I go to this holy place.

When my ex and I separated, I yearned to have intimate time with God. This sanctuary was the only place I had where I would find peace, joy, and a sense that everything was going to turn out okay. It's now become a ritual; every single morning I sit there and have a conversation with God and meditate. It's where I always find my true essence whenever I feel disconnected from my spirit.

I manage and coach all types of personalities who have issues I have to deal with on a daily basis. Asking God to provide me with all the right tools and resources to help me guide them is a must. I know without His help, I would not be getting their very best; I wouldn't even know how to. To be the best me for them can only be done when I spend time in my holy place. It is where my mind, body, and spirit rejuvenate.

As I mentioned earlier, it's also a necessity when it comes to your dating life. As you are going through the course, you need the spirit of discernment to intervene. Trust me, you can't do this on your own, because if you could, you wouldn't be in the predicament you are in now. I'm not judging, I'm speaking from my very own experiences.

There are so many mistakes I could have avoided if I would have first prayed about and meditated on each situation.

There were times I felt God leading me and I ignored Him. Please don't neglect that uncomfortable, uneasy, "something is not right" feeling. Don't question it multiple times, trying to justify what you are sensing in your heart. It is the Holy Spirit speaking to you, and you have to learn how to be confident within yourself in order to walk away from the person. You will have no regrets, but even when you do have moments where your mind is telling you, "Go back or call him," you now have the power to say, "No, I will not go back to what I know in my heart is not for me. I will trust in God's plan for me."

There's a miracle behind every pain and tear. It's hard to see it when you are going through it, but dark seasons come to help us develop. Many times, the spiritual walk will not make sense to the logical mind; in fact, you will doubt yourself. The human brain doesn't operate in God's way, and many things will make you question God's presence. It is normal to feel unease, you will be tested, and you will have to find the answer through meditation and prayer to renew your mind, body, and spirit.

Your faith will keep you going as long you don't let your mind convince you with all sorts of craziness, but when it does, you have to tell your thoughts to shut up. You will get the wishes of your heart, even if they seem impossible. God does the unthinkable, which is what makes Him God. With a world full of negative news, peer pressure, and insecurities, you have to find a place where you can get still. I've come to many of my decisions for the past several years after meditation.

When you pray, you are talking to God, and when you are meditating, you are listening to him; I found this statement to be so profound. There were times I felt like I had gone backwards, to only see after a few months I had moved forward. Being a believer is not about being religious and following religious laws, but it's about knowing Jesus Christ who died to forgive us for our sins and who is a light of love in this world.

I wasn't one to consider meditation until several years ago. I found meditation assists us when we are seeking answers. It allows us to connect with the Creator. When you are always in your head, you don't realize how much internal chaos is happening. The advice I always give my friends when situations occur is don't react. Don't touch it, pray, and meditate so you can get clear instructions on how to move forward. And I have to add that if you don't get an answer right away, it's because you are not supposed to do anything with the situation at the moment.

If you haven't already, I suggest you start implementing these rituals into your daily schedule. It will be life changing and will take your spirituality into a whole different dimension.

It can be challenging giving up power, especially for those who are compulsive controllers. You want to fix everything *now* . . . But when you go into meditation and prayer, you have to surrender to the whole "fixing it," and let God guide you. Certain situations will be a bit convoluted, but understanding why you are waiting on God is what keeps you going.

It's harder when you feel like everyone is surpassing you and getting everything they are asking for from God. It's even tougher when the people you perceive to be "evil" or have "bad energy" are living abundant lives. I've been there, too, and I used to question it as well, until one day it registered that just because they looked like they were getting ahead in life doesn't mean they were doing it with God. God will allow you to do your thing, but it won't last. I've seen so many people who I thought were a lot more fortunate than I—those same people eventually lost it all or were never happy to begin with, since their joy never came from the one who gives complete peace and joy.

You don't want to go ahead of God for a career, love, or anything else you may consider a means of "success." Our ego tries to fool us by saying that if we are not accomplishing our goals by a certain time and of our own accord, we will miss our achievements. But God reminds us what we need to do in Psalm 37:7: "Be still before the Lord and wait patiently for him; do not fret when people succeed in their ways when they carry out their wicked schemes." Our ego won't feel comfortable sitting on the sideline waiting for the right way, but reread the scripture. Don't get impatient and take matters into your hands. I understand many times it won't be clear what God is doing, or if He is even listening, but if you meditate on His word, it will resonate in your soul.

He will give you the tools needed for each step of the way. What I've discovered is God's ways are far beyond our human intelligence. He's always at work, but more than likely it's not going to happen in the form or the time you want it, and He's not always going to answer you the same way He did in the past. Stress is stimulated when we get out of alignment with God's will and try to step into His role, and then get frustrated when our strategy is not working. The best advice I can give you is to stop trying to figure out every detail in your life. You must know what dreams you want to fulfill and be willing to put in the work, but God is the one who handles all the intricacies. We must believe it's already managed in the midst of loneliness or stress.

Pause for a second and pray for God to give you the strength to keep pushing through. Yes, there are some days I feel so invigorated and full of faith and some days I'm questioning everything. It's completely common, and you shouldn't be so hard on yourself. But, you do have to make it a point to snap out of it very quickly. Isaiah 41:10

says, "Fear not, for I am with you; be not dismayed, for I am your God; I will strengthen you, I will help you, I will uphold you with my righteous right hand." He doesn't tell us not to feel fear, because He understands we would be afraid at times, but He says "fear not," which means I know you are scared, but do it afraid. Feelings are very inconsistent. You have to make a conscious decision to do whatever is needed, even if you have to do it afraid.

When we are entirely in the now, we free ourselves from negativity. We let go of how we want our requests to unfold; we let go and let God. The reality is when you think back even to yesterday, it didn't reveal itself exactly how you thought it would, but we are so hectic in our minds we tend not to reflect. You don't have the slightest idea of how God is going to bring your significant other. As you proceed on your meditation path, you will have more clarity in the dating scene. As I mentioned before, you have to pray to God to help you discern if this is the man He's ordained for you, and be ready to let it go once He reveals it—and once He does, don't go searching for what's wrong with you or why he doesn't like you.

First of all, women shouldn't have to be putting in all the work, especially in the beginning. I know it's uncomfortable being single, especially when you've been on the same journey for a while. I also know God is a God of love and joy and He will bring you the one He's ordained for you. I'd been devaluing relationships because of my insecurities. You know what they say when you do the same thing over and over again, but expect different results? It's called *insanity*, my friend.

Life is about self-evaluation and asking God to help you with the things that no longer serve you so that you can become the best you. There's a reason why I feel so strongly about seeing my life unfold the way God needs it to. If my ex had not walked out of my life a couple of years ago, I would've missed my two promotions, the condo I always dreamt of living in, and my brand-new Maserati. And I would have missed the opportunity to travel out to places like Puerto Rico, the Dominican Republic, Dubai, France, South Africa, Iceland, Bali, and Tokyo. Also, I would not have reconnected with amazing girlfriends and met incredible new people.

None of this is to think or feel that material things describe me, but it does bring me a lot of joy and happy tears to see what He has done in just a couple of years. Yes, it hurt a lot when my ex left, but I would never have become the woman I am today, or experienced life with God, if He did not remove my ex. He was showing me, "There's more I have to do with you, and I can't take your ex along." I had to trust it was all happening to allow me to become who I was destined to be.

When my ex walked out, I had two choices: lift my head up and trust that God knew what He was doing, or become the victim and ask, "Why me?" Well, I chose option one, as you can see. There have been seasons in my life when there was nothing but absolute silence. I didn't see a glimpse, not even a bit of hope, that God heard my prayers.

Listen, ladies, I, too, have cried, prayed, and meditated, and I still had no answer at the time I expected. I had to encourage myself to keep going and keep pushing no matter what I was feeling. I would pause for a second and think about all of my present blessings God had already given me. It's great to have people around you encouraging you, but it's even more necessary to be an encourager to yourself. The same God who did it before will be the same God to do it again.

You have to believe when your flesh does not believe it will. Only God knows why you are still in the waiting season. Many of the disciples in the Bible endured hardships before reaping the promise of God. Jesus Christ himself had to endure a tremendous amount of pain to receive His biggest blessing. If you haven't watched the movie

The Passion of the Christ, I suggest you watch it. It's a great reminder that Jesus himself went through a lot to die for our sins. What makes us better than Christ Jesus? We too will have to endure hardships, but your story will end perfectly if you decide not to quit and take whatever you need to cope with to see your blessings manifest.

Don't fall short by letting the devil fool you with tricks. If a guy you've dated in the past contacts you and he's already demonstrated he's not good for you, don't reach back out due to loneliness. A feeling of loneliness can be so detrimental to your progress. You will make decisions you will regret shortly, and then you are back to square one. I'm talking from experience; I've done this a few times, and every time I got so upset with myself for knowing better but doing the opposite. Of course, it didn't go anywhere, and a man shows you who he is from the get-go. Maya Angelou said it correctly: "When someone shows you who they are—believe them." Sometimes since we can't feel or see what God is doing in our lives, we may say, "What the heck, hitting him back up won't hurt." Yes, it will. Don't do it, no matter how lonely you are. I don't care if you are feeling like life sucks and you will never get what you want; this is just crazy stuff we try to convince ourselves of when we are thinking irrationally.

Trust me, ladies, he will eventually let you down by reverting to his old behavior. If things between you and a guy you were talking to, or dating, didn't work out because of his offensive behavior, keep pushing through. God will bring you the man He's ordained for you.

Another great movie is *Miracles from Heaven*. When I watched it, I was crying the entire time. The film is about a little girl who's nine years old and diagnosed with a deadly digestive disease. The little girl had so much faith in God, she kept being tough regardless of the pain she was enduring. Even when hitting her breaking point, she found the strength within herself to continue fighting through it. We all have these moments, and we have to switch our thoughts quickly. The little girl's faith was sincere, she never gave up on God, and she even helped others in the midst of her sickness.

This is exactly what God wants us doing. Stop fretting about whether you will ever meet your husband, have children, or if your career is ever going to happen. He wants us to surrender our weariness to Him and help others while He's taking care of all of our affairs. God always uses our pain for a higher purpose, if you trust Him. If you are hurting right now, faith will get you to finish stronger and better than ever before. God will come into your life and show out.

It doesn't mean disturbances won't be happening in the middle of God working things out. I remember one day receiving a call from a friend letting me know the guy I last dated had proposed to his girlfriend, who was also pregnant by him . . . and to top it off, my ex of four years was also having a baby. I would be lying if I said it didn't hurt. I had all sorts of mixed emotions. I believe the first thing that came out of my mouth was, "Really, God? I've been faithful and holding on tight, but why is it they seem to be getting what I'm requesting from you?" But it wasn't until a few years later when I recognized it wasn't that God was trying to punish me; if anything, He was protecting me. I knew where I was currently in life; I didn't want to be pregnant before marriage. It turned out the last guy and his girlfriend broke up a year later.

We have to thank God for every man He removes from our lives. You will look back one day like I did and say, "Wow, THANK YOU FOR WALKING AWAY, it was a blessing." Of course, you don't know it when it's all happening, but time exposes everything. There's nothing wrong if you've done things out of order in the past. God has already forgiven you. He's a God who's merciful and graceful, but it doesn't mean He's okay with you continuing on the same path. It's time to do things God's way.

Let's be honest with each other—have your yesterdays or current actions worked? They weren't working for me, which is why I shed off my old self and became the person I knew God created me to be. There's a particular order required when you are walking in God's light. Trust me; I didn't know this before my breakup. I don't even know if I knew this a year after the breakup, but I eventually was spiritually awakened by the many hard knocks life kept throwing at me due to my lack of obedience and the many life tests I wasn't passing. I was ready to be obedient! I was tired of repeating the same vicious cycle over and over again. I refused to resume going on the same route, or even worse, settle for a life less than what God created me to have. Oh, heck nah, I will not be living a mediocre life just to live up to society's standards.

It saddens me to see where our generation and future generations are heading. All you have to do is look at social media to see the number of women who are exposing their bodies just for a "like." Really? Is selling your soul for men's approval worth it? Believe it or not, a God-fearing man is not looking for those types of qualities in a wife. Don't get fooled by what you see, but behave and dress the way you want to be treated. Be classy, be smart, be a go-getter, be what God designed you to be, and before you know it, your Prince Charming will be sent to you by God.

God will never give us an assignment which He hasn't already gone ahead of us and won. He knows the beginning and the end. Don't be afraid to take the risk of letting go of everything you've been doing that is not bringing you the results you are seeking. Ask God to show you the way, but you have to be obedient. If this means letting go of everyone and everything, do it. I can tell you the feeling of loneliness will arise, but this is a space you have to get to and be comfortable in to see God's fullness in your life. The season of quietness will reveal where your current state of mind is and what proper steps you need to take for your next chapter.

Many women get afraid of loneliness to only end up in the arms of someone who is going to leave them not only empty again, but newly insecure.

It took me a very long time to comprehend what it meant to be in a chapter in your life when you have no one around but feel the most joy, peace, and fullness within. A feeling that everything I'm praying for is here now, in my heart. I used to think the great gurus who talked about such a place were just crazy and looney. I was the crazy one . . . I was the one not accepting God's best into my life. I was the one frightened of being by myself, so I allowed men who I knew God hadn't ordained for me into my heart. The Word says in Proverbs 4:23, "Watch over your heart with all diligence, for from it flow the springs of life."

We are going around giving our hearts out to almost every man that comes into our lives. Our poor little souls, the amount of stress we put them through for unnecessary reasons. There are just certain situations God tells us from the beginning not to step into, but we ignore our gut, and then wonder why they end in heartbreak. Don't be stubborn when the soft voice called the Holy Spirit is leading you. Listen to it no matter how hard the decision is to pull the plug from a relationship. It will save you pain and time, plus it will get you closer to the one God has for you.

God doesn't ask us to change our lives for Him, but for ourselves. He knows if we proceed with our current behavior, it's only going to end up in destruction. He wants us to have an abundant life, our days flowing with peace and joy. But if you maintain a life that you know at your core is not your true essence, you will never receive your full inheritance. God can't give you a blessing if you are too occupied holding on to old things. Free your hands and let go of all the garbage holding you back from receiving your benefits. Accept where you are in life right now and decide to start making changes. You are responsible for your being. Life is what you make it! And if you end up on your deathbed without accomplishing everything you knew you were destined to be, it's no one's fault but yours.

Be confident and know your worth, my Queen. There's a great quote that says, "Raise your standards, and the universe will meet you there." It's the law of attraction—you attract who you are. Refuse to live an unhappy life, make a declaration that you will be obedient and do whatever is necessary to love yourself the way you deserve to be loved. Remember, you treat yourself the way you want others to treat you. To be treated like a queen, you need to see your worth. It has nothing to do with the outer, but how you feel internally. Do you see yourself the way God sees you? You are number one in God's eyes, don't ever let anyone every treat you like you're anything less.

CHAPTER EIGHT

PURE SILENCE

Have you ever found yourself in just pure silence? And what I mean is when you feel like nothing is happening. When some days are just extremely quiet, and you can't make out what God is doing in your life. When moments like these occur, which they will, if you aren't paying attention you can quickly revert to your old ways, especially when you don't see the light at the end of the tunnel.

The best solution when you are having moments like these is to listen to a guided meditation on gratitude. When you focus on everything that is going great in your life, the fear of the unknown will vanish. You can't be in the state of gratitude and fear at the same time; it's impossible. Many times, we concentrate on what's going wrong or what's missing in our lives, and we tend to forget what is going right. Youtube has some great twenty-minute guided gratitude videos, which are great to start with until you can do it by yourself. Another great exercise is to write down three to five things you are grateful for toward the end of the night before going to bed.

If you have been on this journey for a while, you will find yourself questioning if you will ever be married or if your prayers are being heard. You have to hold tight, girlfriend. Remember, you are waiting on God's best and that may take some time. God has to get you and your future husband right before He brings the union together. You have to let go of whatever timeframe you've given yourself, let go of the outcome, and believe God will make a way.

There have been times when I've heard my girlfriends say, "I need to get out more often to find my husband," so everywhere we hangout they are on the lookout for "the one." Ladies, I don't believe this is how God works. You don't ever have to go looking for him. You have to step out and be present, which means being out with your friends and enjoying your time with them. You know what happens when you go out with the expectations to meet a man and it doesn't happen?

You will be disappointed and go home sad, feeling lonelier than ever and having missed out on spending "present time" with your girls. You may want to text the last guy who walked away from you, and we all know what the outcome of that text will be. Now, that's what we call insanity. Don't continue replicating the vicious cycle. You won't improve or become who you were designed to be if you are not willing to give up what you've always done in the past. Rewrite your story—you are the author of your destiny. Yes, there will be things that happen in between, but you are capable and able to handle whatever life throws at you.

Let me fully warn you: it will be hard because we are creatures of habit. You have to go against everything your negative thoughts are telling you to do. You have to go beyond your comfort zone to head towards your calling. Know where you are going. Pain is temporary, and it will subside, but you have to take the first step. Don't go around being the victim, trying to get people to feel sorry for you. Be courageous and strong. Do the necessary steps to take your life in a whole different direction. Don't do what is easy, do what will bring you the most significant rewards. Always go to God in prayer for guidance about someone you just met, or even when a relationship has ended.

God will give you the strength and mindset needed to do what is needed next. You have no idea how many times I've prayed to God about someone I just met. I would tell God I was surrendering this person to Him and ask Him to show me each step of the way, but if this person was not for me, to remove him.

I will tell you again—God will remove people from your life if they're not part of His grand plan for you, and you can't be running after the person when God shuts the door. Don't try to reopen it or beg God to bring the person back. Let things go no matter what, and have faith God will bring you someone better.

I've seen it over and over again in my life and will tell you that God never gives you less than your past. It's when I've settled that I experienced less than God's best due to the despair of being alone. It never works at the end of the day.

There will be days you need to take time to ponder where you are currently and where you want to go. A walk on the beach or walking on the treadmill always get me to think in the present about things that need correction. This also helps me to see how far I've come from the moment I commenced holding myself accountable to the life I wanted to live. Solitary moments are instrumental for self-improvement.

I knew when I began the journey to self-awareness I needed to develop patience and learn how to go with the flow instead of trying to force outcomes. I can sense I would get impatient with myself and God when I felt like my prayers were going unheard, or I couldn't understand what God was doing with me. I came up with 5/5/5/5/5 to help me in this area.

1. Five Minutes of Gratitude

2. Five Minutes of Prayers

3. Five Minutes Visualization

4. Five Minutes of Meditation

5. Five Minutes of Affirmations.

It's a total of twenty-five minutes devoted to help you jump start your day intentionally.

I also read the Bible for a few minutes each day. I know many of God's people in the Bible endured pain and afflictions but still succeeded in their patience and faith, no matter how painful their experiences were. Next, I listen to motivational videos first thing in the morning while working out. I wanted to rewire my brain to think positively instead of expecting the worst. I would watch motivational videos while I was getting ready for and commuting to work. It would get my creative juices and my endorphins going, acting as a great jumpstart in the daylight. Habits can form in thirty days, so I did this consistently for a month.

You have to encourage yourself when things that you didn't expect to happen in your life begin happening. Again, I knew God had a purpose behind my ex walking away and my tumor diagnosis, but I also knew if my negative thinking took over, I could get discouraged and start a pity party. Who in the world wants to start their day this way? I've even had self-talks, saying, "Angelina, listen here, you better get it together, you will not allow yourself to play the victim. You will overcome this, and not only will you overcome it, you will become better because of it. Control your thoughts, now." Yes, I sure did have conversations with myself while looking at my bedroom mirror.

Trust me when I tell you, you will not attract anyone worthy into your life with a bad attitude or negative energy. This is why taking time to reflect on any immediate actions you need to take to improve your attitude is so important. Many times, we don't take notice, but when someone we were deeply in love with turns their back on us, it can harden our hearts. If you don't handle it right away, it will get rooted deep in your spirit, and it will be extremely difficult to get past the pain when you reach this point.

When I would have moments of reflections, I would notice my surroundings. I observed a tremendous amount of people allowing their circumstances to darken their light. They looked like walking zombies, letting their situations determine their moods. I consciously decided not to be one of them. It's not being judgmental, but being present and knowing what you want to experience. Don't let yourself get caught up in your emotions, because that's exactly what they are—emotions. Emotions come and go.

You are a fearless individual and have all the power within to overcome and become everything you set out to become. You were made in the image of God, our Creator of the entire universe. I remind myself of this every day. If God is in me, that means I can do all things through Christ who strengthens me. When you reach your awakening moment, two questions you should ask our Heavenly Father are, "What is my reason for being here on earth?" and "How can I be the best me?"

I've met so many angels along my journey, especially during my health struggles. God has shown me that miracles still exist and are happening every second of our lives. I met wonderful, loving people who I would have never crossed paths with if it wasn't for the tumor. There have been other folks who have either touched my life or I have touched theirs.

God also rekindled old friendships with people who helped me during my heartbreak. There are so many people who have prayed for my healing. I mean, there were moments I would show up at Jackson Memorial Hospital and everyone—and I mean literally almost everyone—would be looking for me. It felt so surreal. They would give me hugs and encourage me with comforting words. God was the only possible answer for all I was encountering. I know nothing happens by chance; He orchestrated every move before I even got there. God was giving me winks every step of the way. He was demonstrating I had nothing to fear, for He was with me and never left me. I just needed to worry less and trust more.

Are you living or worrying? Many of us are missing out on what life has to offer us because we are so concerned about our futures. We miss out on all the great moments that are happening right now, which we can never get back because we are so busy in our heads. We are worried and filled with all kinds of questions. Why am I single? Am I ever going to get married? Am I ever going to get a great paying career? Am I going to have kids? And the list goes on and on and on.

We put an enormous amount of pressure on ourselves, when in reality life is mysterious and all we have is right now. Do your best with where you are and with what you have, and let God handle the details. Are you asking me how in the world you are supposed to do this? Well, first realize you are now worried about another question— just kidding. But seriously, the answer is really simple and it's all been written in the Bible.

It's called faith, and without it, it will be tough to get through this thing we call life. For example, if you are ready to be in a relationship but God removes the guy you are "kicking it" with, you have the option to trust that God is saving you from a heartbreak, or you can pout and throw a tantrum because you feel God is not answering your prayers. You have to know that silent seasons mean you are sowing seeds. Don't gripe in quiet moments when nothing seems to be happening; just tell yourself, "I'm sowing my seed, I will soon be receiving my harvest."

During your sowing season, you will meet men that we can call "players." Don't waste your time or grow weary with men you know are not the one. Remove diversions and continue focusing on what you prayed for. You will get to a place in your life where you can identify these clowns from a mile away. What you need to do now is prepare yourself to receive the person God has ordained for you. You do this by living life to the fullest. Start doing what you've always wanted to do: travel the world, hang with friends, work out consistently, pray, meditate . . . Believe everything is working itself out, and you are going to enjoy your life to its current capacity until God presents his promise to you.

Too many of us are walking around unhappy and bitter because we don't have a significant other. Here's a little secret, no one can complete you but God. If you are feeling empty now, when you get into a relationship and the honeymoon phase fizzles away, you will be back in the place of emptiness. Focus on you . . . Surround yourself with people who are going to support you on this journey.

Just have fun and enjoy the present moment. Life is truly short, and tomorrow is not guaranteed, so why waste it on things you can't control? You can look at a curve ball and feel defeated or look at the same ball and throw it back even harder. Life is what you make it. Yes, things will happen that will throw you off your game and make you feel like you have failed. But don't believe your mind's lies. It may be your current reality, but it doesn't determine where and what God is going to do in your life.

If you are firm and steadfast with whatever obstacle comes your way, you will be surprised both by what you can accomplish and what you become. It took me a while to get to this point. I'm helping you avoid depression, confusion, loneliness, and worry and to live life the way God intended you to live it. Growth only happens when our back is against the wall.

CHAPTER NINE

WHO ARE YOU RECEIVING ADVICE FROM?

Be very cautious about who you get your advice from. Many women seek guidance from other women who have no idea how to run their own lives. Before asking a girlfriend for her input, you need to evaluate where she is in her current life. It is not to be judgmental, but the word does say in I Corinthians 15:33, "Do not be misled: 'Bad company corrupts good character.'" Be cautious of your inner circle; who you hang with is you who become.

Here are a few questions I ask myself first before seeking advice. Would I like to imitate this person's behavior? Is this person a spiritual survivor, able to go through life's storms encouraged by and trusting in God? And, most importantly, is my spirit at peace when I am having a conversation about my problem? I'm still a firm believer in speaking to God about my situation first. I understand sometimes you need to vent to a friend, but pay attention to whose opinions you are seeking. Remember, at the end of the day this person should be praying for you and not leading you into more destructive behaviors, leaving your spirit feeling worse than before.

Also, go to God in pure silence. As I mentioned before, it will be the most uncomfortable feeling at first, but with practice, your mind will learn to be still. You are the one in control of your mind. The moment you make being silent for a few minutes a priority in order to get clarity or to renew your mind, silence will become a ritual and take your inner being to higher heights in the spiritual realm.

The reason why it benefits you to be in silence for a few minutes a day is because our nature is to always overthink our future. We get afraid and create unnecessary stress and fear. Taking a few deep breaths throughout the day is essential. You may even find yourself not needing to vent to anyone. God will give a knowing peace that everything is going to work out. God whispers and never yells or forces Himself on us. If you are always on the go or find yourself emotionally distressed a majority of the time, it's even more necessary to find time to spend with God. Many of your friends are going through their own troubles, so their advice won't reasonably be the best, but if needed, God will bring you the right person to vent to. You will know it in your spirit when the person has been sent your way to help you through a particular situation. I also suggest hiring a coach in the area you are seeking growth in. I have found that having an impactful coach in your life will help you push forward and, most importantly, help you live with purpose.

Read books from authors who have had success in the area you are trying to improve in. Feed your spirit with people and resources that are going to elevate you spiritually. Find successful couples to interview. Why not ask questions? What's made their marriage so fortunate? What's the one thing you can take away from the couple, and the one thing you should not do in a marriage? Prepare yourself to be a wife before you become one.

Be vigilant with the types of music you are exposing yourself in the growing and silent seasons. Music is the theater of the mind. If you are listening to love songs or heartbreak songs, you will start to feel emotional. Surrounding your spirit with uplifting music, ambiance, or even friends will get your energy flowing in the right direction. Worship music and motivational videos on YouTube were vital to my silent season. They encouraged me and kept me going in my weakest moments. I never understood why some women surrounded themselves with somber music or negative people when going through a rough time.

It's mental suicide, and it will screw your head up. Don't make the heartbreak, or whatever you may be going through, harder than it already is. Instead, thank the man who decided to walk away from your life so now you can work on becoming who you were destined to be. In your quiet season, you have to consider what new experiences you want to attract into your life. Take advice from people who have gone through the storm and came out stronger and better.

CHAPTER TEN

SOCIAL MEDIA

Oh yes, let us talk about it! It just saddens my heart to see the amount of mess circulating through social media. You are looking at your life thinking it sucks because you keep comparing it to what you see on social media. There are so many women and men that are sharing an illusion of a fabricated life.

Ladies, 90 percent of what you see on Instagram, Facebook, Twitter, Snapchat, or whatever other social media platforms you are on is not authentic. I found this out to be true by just observing the people at work or around me. I see one of my friends taking pictures with her husband, vacationing somewhere looking like they have a perfect marriage, when I know her husband is cheating. Now, if I didn't truly know this friend, all I would see is a happy marriage. And don't get me wrong, I know there are authentic happy marriages, but what I am saying is don't get caught in the hype of what you see.

You are scrolling through the pics wondering why all these women are in relationships and you are not. You start questioning your worth and your hope. Don't let photos throw you off your game. Sometimes when we expose ourselves to these types of platforms, they can do us more harm than good. If you find your soul drained by the time you go through your timeline, it means the people you are following are not elevating your spirit, and it is time to unfollow them.

It seems like women are getting more and more desperate to elevate their value based on how many "likes" they get and will go to extreme measures to get as many likes and followers as possible. Please don't be that woman who's posting half-naked pictures. I have found the women who take pictures of their bodies—butt and boob shots— are the ones who are dealing with the most insecurities. I know you are thinking that they are the ones getting all the men "liking" their pictures, and you are correct. Men will follow and like their images, but for all the wrong reasons. All they are thinking about is, "How can I hit that?" And most importantly, why would you want a man who was only attracted to you because you were half-naked?

If you are asking God for marriage, you need to behave like a lady at all times. Is it me, or are many of the women posting such foolishness usually the ones who are single anyway? Don't get caught up in the hype, and make a conscious decision to live your own life. I mentioned this before, but let's be real—do you want to be exposing your body for the world to see? What exactly are you trying to accomplish by doing this? Could it be a void you are trying to fill? I don't care how many likes you get; you will never fill the void by the number of likes you get on social media.

The emptiness you are encountering is coming from something so much more profound, and only God can fill it in.

Do you need a man to determine if you are beautiful or not? You need to know you were beautifully and wonderfully made from the moment you came into this world. Don't go buying a counterfeit body to get men's approval; if you do want to get surgery, do it for you and not for others. When you do things for others, it takes away from you being 100 percent authentic, which is what makes you so unique.

You should be gratified and welcome every part of your body from head to toe. You are flawless just the way you are, and don't let anyone else tell you otherwise.

Be selective about who you are following on social media. Stay away from things that will make you feel less than. There are a ton of inspirational and motivating people who you can start following. If you are stalking your ex on social media, immediately unfollow him. Do not follow any person you've dated and you have no communication with. It is none of your business what's happening in their life. It's time to clean your closet and start with a new slate. You are focusing on the now and preparing for the future.

Do me a favor: take ten minutes to unfollow people who you know are not feeding your soul with positive energy. And how do you distinguish if they're helpful or harmful vibes? By what you observe in your stomach and heart when you come across their posts. Does it feel good, or all of a sudden do you feel uneasy about your current life? Do not flounder; this is your life. Stop reading, go to all of your social media handles, and unfollow the foolishness and exes that you are currently following.

Doesn't it feel great when you have taken the first step in eliminating anything that doesn't serve you? What I can tell you is you will be tempted to follow them again. Remember, it takes about thirty days to break a habit. After the thirty days, gauge how you are feeling—more than likely you will be feeling somewhat relieved to have detached yourself from your old erratic actions. Remember, you are striving to become the best version of yourself. Specific behaviors from antiquity can't come along on your new journey.

Ladies, please be cautious not to post anything that you will regret later. Don't follow the trend of the naked bodies, trying to be the flavor of the month. I hope you noticed the word "trying," because it won't work. It's like someone who gets high on cocaine for the first time; they go back to it, trying to get the feeling they got the first time, failing to realize they will never get that high again. I know I used a deep analogy, but hopefully you get the point.

Social media is an addiction and can lead you on the wrong path if you don't know who you are. You will post an X-rated picture, get a ton of likes, which will make you feel popular, which equates to wanting to be accepted and loved. It is all temporary and superficial, all driven by ego, and before you know it you've now become "one of them." Just like the group of women who will do whatever is necessary to get the attention they are seeking, you will fail to realize God is the only one who can give you everything you want to obtain. Please don't get caught up—be selective in what you post. You can still be sexy and classy. You don't have to sell your soul to get "likes." Use the platform to elevate other people by showcasing the crafts God gave you specifically, and I'm pretty sure your talent is NOT showing your boobs and butt.

You were not brought into this world to be mediocre and suffer all the time. Stop comparing yourself to others. Today's society gives the impression that material things or money are the most important aspects of life. This couldn't be farther from the truth. God wants you to live an abundant life, but this doesn't mean your self-worth is contingent on what someone else has. True happiness is when you can be comfortable with who God created you to be. If you take control of your mind, you will realize you are unique, created in God's image, flawlessly made. Pay attention to what interests you gravitate to; this is your purpose. There's a distinctive calling explicitly designed for you.

Trust me, if you don't follow your calling, God will send someone else. Don't scroll through Instagram, Facebook, or Snapchat wishing to have someone else's life. First of all, you don't know what they had to endure to be who they are and have what they have. Are you willing to pay the price? Secondly, and most importantly, you lose who you are and what you were destined to be without realizing you are trying to copy someone else's life. How sad is that? You will end up depressed because there will be an empty void until you are walking in your truth.

When you are going after everything you know in your heart God destined you to have, you have now become a leader and not a follower. Run your race! Yes, I'm screaming this out loud to you because I've seen so many women who are insecure, and it stems from following the crowd and comparing themselves with other women. It's the worst thing you can do. God has made each one of us unique. You may resemble someone, but you will never look one hundred percent like someone else or vice versa. And, honestly speaking, why would you want to look like someone else?

This social media generation is growing more and more precarious. People are constantly looking at the posts that aren't even ninety percent of how people are actually living. Ladies, know you were made extraordinary and uncommon for a reason. You don't need to get a bunch of cosmetic surgery to make you feel pretty. You are beautiful just the way you are! Have you ever seen a good-looking man married to what you may consider a not so attractive woman? It is probably because the woman has so much confidence in who she is. It seems the prettier the girl is, the more self-esteem issues she has.

I can't comprehend this, but I do remember in my twenties feeling the pressure of having to keep up with what society called "beautiful." As I continued growing in Christ, I quickly realized those women I identified as "beautiful" were the same ones dealing with emptiness and depression. They exuded confidence from the outside, but the moment they opened their mouths, their words were superficial. And what I was exploring was confidence that radiated from within me and would radiate outward.

I started affirming my truth, which is that I'm God's daughter—He made me perfect. I AM BEAUTIFUL and FEARLESSLY MADE! I didn't get to this point overnight; it took effort from my end to make sure I was spending time in God's word. I wanted to know everything God made me to be and not believe society's lies. I wanted real joy coming from within.

Yes, I love fashion, designer brands, and make-up. I'm the typical girly girl, but I also know none of those things can make me happy or define me. You can get a new bag, and a few months later, it doesn't make you as excited as when you first got it. Maybe now you go and get a new outfit, but again, a few months later it doesn't have the same effect. It's because these things don't bring genuine joy. I spent a lot of my energy and resources searching for happiness, when all along it was already in me; I just had to tap into it. I was dating guys who I knew weren't the ones God would want me with; I was chasing the wrong people and things.

Much of the advice I've given you is based on my own adventures. I've evolved in so many ways, but the best evolution is when I figured out why I came into this world. I experienced a lot of twists and turns, but I found my purpose by not following the trend and doing some serious soul-searching. Comparing my life to the lives of others wasn't going to help me find my "why" in life, so I became very selective of the people I surrounded myself with, the books I was reading, the places I was going, and what I exposed my eyes to. I focused on channeling my energy into actions aligned with my "why."

The strangest thing was that none of these things happened while I was with my ex-boyfriend.

It's like a light bulb switched on the day he walked away. I'm not even sure if I would have done any soul-searching if it wasn't for the breakup. I used every tear that came down from my eye to push me more and more to my calling. Yes, it hurt while I was growing, but our growing years are supposed to be painful. It is what you do with the pain that determines the outcome of your next chapter. God works miracles in the most mysterious ways.

I'm hoping you are taking my advice so you don't have to take the long, strenuous road. You will start attracting the people you need and begin living life to its fullest. Yes, there will be some lows, but you will look at them differently. You will view them as growth events and not pain. You will understand that if God permitted it to come your way, it's because there's a teaching in the rain. It's up to you on how long you want to stand in the rain. I've had some atrocious seasons, but when I look back, there was nothing I couldn't have handled. Life is still great regardless of the barriers I've confronted and the future ones coming.

CHAPTER ELEVEN

ANOTHER CURVEBALL

What to do when you've been thrown another curveball in the middle of trying to survive a heartbreak?

As I have detailed throughout this book, I was devastated and didn't know how to register being diagnosed with a tumor. My spirit got depressed, and I wasn't sure where God was at that moment or why He would allow this to happen, especially when I was already dealing with so much. This chapter is on how to juggle life's storms without letting them break you. How do you build endurance when life seems to be falling apart?

It happened to me on September 27, 2017, the day after my birthday, when I had barely gotten out of the fire and now I was being thrown into another furnace. Months prior, I started to see a shift on my face by my right nostril. I went to see different specialists, but they said it was only a small lesion. I do recall an unsettling feeling within—I knew something wasn't right, so I started researching my symptoms on my own. I even went to a natural healer, but I sensed it was beyond the holistic stage.

It was no surprise when I found out I had a health issue, but I wasn't expecting it to be a tumor. A tumor that, if I didn't remove it within sixty days, would cause me to lose my gums, bones, teeth, and ability to speak. Now, this was probably one of the most traumatic moments of my life.

I had to fight the good fight of faith. Life was testing me at every angle you could think of, but it was up to me not to give up and to continue doing whatever was necessary to see the victory. I told myself this didn't catch God off guard, which meant He would get me through it. Yes, there were moments I would break down in tears. Life is going to hit you with bricks, and if you don't know how to build a secure house with the bricks thrown at you, you will develop a home without a firm foundation that will eventually fall apart.

A week after removing the tumor from my face, I was depressed, but the sadness brought me to a place of asking great questions. I started interrogating what I wanted out of life. What's my real purpose in this world, anyway? All of a sudden, I went from a victim mentality to determined to use this detrimental experience for good. Just maybe everything that was happening was to bring me to this very moment of asking myself profound soul-searching questions. Keeping it real, I never asked myself any of these questions until my health dilemma. We all know life has all types of peaks and valleys, but it is in when you are in the valley that you find out how tough you are.

Every single experience you are going through has to happen. If you try to go around it, you will only be delaying the lesson you are supposed to learn or the growth required for your next chapter. You will stay in the same place until you make a conscious decision to do what you need to do with a positive attitude. There isn't a shortcut in life. Pass the test! Don't let circumstances define you. Tell yourself over and over again, "I can do all things through Christ who strengthens me."

Remember, when you focus on your life—even in your lowest moments, moments of darkness when you feel like nothing is going right—that's when things are shifting for you. It may not happen right away; in fact, it may even get worse, but if you keep your faith and believe, you will see your status change for good. Decide you will live your life and run your race. Use this quiet time to talk to God. Romans 15:4 says, "Such things were written in the Scriptures long ago to teach us. And the Scriptures give us hope and encouragement as we wait patiently for God's promises to manifest." God has given instructions in the Bible. It is so important to spend time reading God's manual.

It took me a while to get this point, but now when I read the Word, I'm just in awe of the sum of information and life lessons that are in it. It does give hope, and it encourages me to keep going. I will tell you the biggest thing for me to learn was patience. Oh, how I sucked when it came to waiting for anything too long. I would go ahead of God all the time. Lack of self-control is what probably caused many heartaches, trials, and tribulations. If it didn't happen fast enough, I would figure out how to fix it, which, of course, only led me to more turmoil.

The Bible speaks so much about patience, but it wasn't until I started spending quality time with God and in His word that I learned about the importance of being obedient to the word. The Scripture says in I Samuel 15:22, "But Samuel replied, 'What is more pleasing to the LORD: your burnt offerings and sacrifices or your obedience to his voice? Listen! Obedience is better than sacrifice, and submission is better than offering the fat of rams.'" I know, I was shaken, too, when I read this passage. I would pretty much pick and choose the areas I found convenient until God checked me one day. It was either I was going to go all in or not at all.

Another great scripture to help you to get through this season is in Psalm 37:5, "Commit your way to the LORD; trust in him, and he will act." I do not know about you, but these words bring me so much peace. We have a Heavenly Father saying that all we have to do is commit all of our days to Him, and He will act on our behalves. Isn't this wonderful? You do not have to go trying to compromise who you are to get your ideal gig or to have a man in your life. God is going to do it for you. You have to be willing to wait for Him and not grump while He is handling your affairs.

If you are feeling trapped, it could be because you haven't given your life entirely to God. Is there an area in your life you haven't yielded to the Lord? What exactly are you doing at this current moment in your life to demonstrate that you are all in with God? Luke 11:36 says, "If you are filled with light, with no dark corners, then your whole life will be radiant, as though a floodlight were filling you with light." Check to see if there are any dark corners you haven't fully committed to letting go so that God can shine His radiant light over your entire life.

Do you think God would intentionally withhold the blessings He has for you? There are lessons before every blessing. The more you resist something, the more it will persist. Believe and surrender it all to God; He is handling all of your affairs. In the meantime, as I said, you have to work on yourself. Don't try to rush the process or even think God needs your slightest help. God does not need our guidance; in fact, He says, "Be still and know that I am God." You have to believe what He is doing is more you can ever achieve on your own.

Remember, we are continuously evolving, and if we base our feelings and needs on where we are in life right now, we will be making some horrific emotional decisions. God knows where He wants you in your career and love life in the next three, five, and ten years. Even when it gets bumpy, you have to fasten your seat belt, knowing you will arrive at your destination safely and on time.

Another great word to stand on when there are many moving parts in your life and you have no idea where they are all leading you is in Proverbs 3:5, "Trust in the LORD with all your heart; do not depend on your understanding." It is not always going to make sense to you. In fact, I have discovered the more sense it makes to your logical mind, the more you have excluded God. You have to remember, God's ways are so much higher than yours. You cannot even fathom the love God has for you. How in the world are you also going to understand His ways? If you did, you would not be worried or anxious about anything because you would know He will handle it.

Have you loved and trusted someone and knew they loved and trusted you as well? If your answer is yes, you probably didn't question anything that came from their mouth, or if they would let you down. Imagine if you put that amount of trust and undeniable faith in the one who created you? How would your world look? Would you be worried about your future outcome? Of course not. However, luckily God knew we ran short in this area and gave us His grace and mercy. One thing I know for certain is He will grant us our dreams and desires. Even if they do not happen exactly how you thought they should, they will—and even better than you expected.

When I was tested regarding my tumor, I had two options: continue with the "why me" mentality or snap out of it, stand on God's word—"I can handle all things through Christ who strengthens me"—and fight back even harder. I chose the second option; I refused to let the news destroy my inner spirit. I remembered Proverbs 31:25 says, "She is clothed with strength and dignity; she can laugh at the days to come." I decided to face it with a positive mindset. I told a few of my prayer warriors, and they prayed as I was going through one of the most painful moments in my life.

The reason I share this chapter with you is to let you know some of us will have to face multiple oppositions at the same time. It is hard, no doubt, but whenever God does such things, it is because He knows you can handle them. It is easy to walk around excited about your life when everything is going your way, but what happens when fate is probing you over and over again? Do you quit and feel like God has abandoned you? No, you keep going! You do whatever is necessary to continue pushing through to become even stronger than before.

In the moments you find yourself disputing the path you are on, you have to remember what God says in Deuteronomy 31:8, "The LORD himself goes before you and will be with you; he will never leave you nor forsake you. Do not be afraid; do not be discouraged." He already said He would go ahead of you, so you have no reason to fear.

Even though I did not know how everything was going to unfold, and I had moments that fear crept in, I kept God's words close to my heart. I would encourage myself and remind myself that God has the final say. It kept me going in my lowest times.

I jotted down where I envisioned the incision being. I didn't want it to be visible, and for some odd reason, I kept holding the right side of my hip when I pictured my scar. The doctors kept saying they would have to cut the right side of my leg for a blood vessel needed for my mouth. I refused to accept what they were suggesting; I couldn't see myself with an enormous cut on my leg. And to add to the madness, they also said they would have to cut the lower right side of my face. I prayed every morning and night and said my affirmations out loud, drilling what I was picturing into my subconscious.

When I went to my follow-up appointment a few weeks later, the doctor gave me other options. Well, let me tell you in detail God's work at the doctor's appointment. As I was waiting in the room, my doctor, along with a team of other doctors, entered. They were reviewing my case and my doctor turned to me to say, "Angelina, we don't have a choice and we will need to proceed with the leg." I choked up and excused myself from the room to go to the restroom. I was in the bathroom praying out loud, saying "Lord, I surrender. I've done all I can do from my end. It sucks that there's not another alternative, but if this is your will for me, it is what it is." I genuinely surrendered, wiped my tears, and went back to the room.

As I was sitting there, another doctor who had always been working on my case walked in and asked them the game plan. When they told her, she said, "She's too young—there has to be another solution." All of the sudden, the doctor who removed the tumor recommended maybe taking the blood vessel from the upper right side of my shoulder. I felt joyful tears coming from my eyes, and in a matter of minutes, it went from only one way to another possibility, where the scar would be less apparent. God came into the room and handled business. I knew it was God all day! Even though it turned out even better, my surgery ended up being on my right hip bone. I knew from that moment on I had nothing to worry about because God was controlling every detail of my surgery.

Ladies, life will toss you around if you let it and leave your wondering where God is in the center of it all. I promise He is right next to you, holding you by your right hand and carrying you through it all. You have to commit to believing in Him no matter what comes your way. Even when none of it makes sense, you keep going, assuming He is going to open the right door at the perfect time. People are watching you. Are you going to break and let the naysayers and spectators be right? No, you fight back with the word of God. You stand on the truth and keep pressing. Psalm 138:3 says, "On the day I called, You answered me; You made me bold with strength in my soul."

Don't be too hard on yourself when you have weak moments; if you could do this walk on your own, you would not need God. In moments of despair when you are about to shatter, you have to call upon His name. He will do what you cannot handle; He gives rest to the weary. Every time I had the urge to break down I would say, "Jesus, help me—my spirit has weakened, and I need your strength to keep going." There's power in His name. He never failed me. Every time I blurted out, "Jesus; I need you," I would feel his presence.

When you are thrown into the burning furnace again, do not get alarmed, my friend. For God never gives you more than you can handle. He gives the biggest and hardest battles to his most reliable soldiers. First Corinthians 10:13 says, "No temptation has seized you except what is common to man. Moreover, God is faithful; he will not let you be tempted beyond what you can bear. However, when you are tempted, he will also provide a way out so that you can stand up under it." He is not giving you more than you can bear. If He allowed it to happen, it's because He knows you have already won the battle, and He knows you have everything in you to win this spiritual war.

Do you believe you do? It takes two to make it happen. God cannot do it for you. He will carry you through, but you have to be willing to fight this baby out with faith. You, too, have to believe it in your heart; you are a winner. You can handle this and anything else that tries to knock you down. Les Brown said it perfectly: "When life knocks you down, try to land on your back because if you can look up, you can get up."

People usually give up when they are at the edge of a breakthrough. God did not bring you this far to bring you only this far. This is not how our Creator works. He wants you to achieve the impossible in your life so others can believe in Him. There are times people forget how much God has already done in their lives and get caught up in what is not working in their present lives.

It takes you being appreciative of what He has already done to be able to look beyond your current circumstances. Sometimes just pausing for a second to see all the beauty around you allows you to see how amazing God is. I know it sounds very hokey pokey, but it works. You have to get out of your mind and not let your thoughts take over. If you stop and tell your brain, "You will not control this moment or my future," and start to think of all the good that is happening, you will surely find a few things to be grateful about.

When I did this exercise, it quickly took my mind off the tumor. It allowed me to see that life wasn't all that bad. Yes, the reality was I was going through a health issue and didn't have any idea at the time how I was going to overcome it, but I knew our Heavenly Father did. I started to pause after I said thank you for a specific blessing, to feel it in my heart. I realized even with the tumor, many folks are praying their hearts out for the life that I have.

It is a conscious decision you have to make. The mind was created only to survive, and when you are in a state of anxiety, it will go into flight mode. You have to make a habit of being grateful for all the small things occurring in your life. It does not matter if it is as little as enjoying a cup of coffee. Minuscule grateful moments will add up to great ones. You will not know exactly when or how it happened, but you will start to feel joy in your heart, even when you are going through a growing pain season.

November 16th was my surgery date. I remember going into the hospital with a butterfly feeling in my stomach, but also with this peace within that surpassed my human understanding. I knew God had me in the palm of His hand. I felt safe, and He provided me with the most supportive and loving family and friends. When the doctor came into the pre-operative room to mark the areas they would be cutting, I asked if there was any way to avoid cutting the side of my lower face. He said he was afraid not and would try his best to make the incision as thin as possible. I was also being cut in my hip bone to remove a bone and a blood vessel, and was told I would have a scar from my upper side boob all the way to my pelvic section.

I did all I could do to "surrender." I had prayed for eleven months, asking God only to let it be one incision in the least visible place on the body. Prayers are powerful! When I woke up in ICU, I remember the first thing I did was touch my face to feel how thick and long my cut was. My sister asked me what I was doing, and I told her I was feeling to see how severe the damage to my face was.

God responded to my prayers. I had no scar on my face or right leg. I only had one scar on the right side of my hip bone. *God is real!* He answered my prayer. Right before the team of doctors took me into the surgery room, I put on my headset, held my rosary, and listened to gospel music. I surrendered to "what is," and fully trusted God knew what He was doing.

To this day I get emotional in seeing how God worked out every detail of my surgery and did more than I even asked for. If God does not remove the situation, He will carry you through it. This testimony is to give you hope in case you are in a perplexed season. Be brave, pray BOLD, and have confidence that God will acknowledge you. If He does not give you precisely what you petitioned for, it is because He has something much better in mind.

Pray without ceasing. Prayer is powerful; this is the way we communicate with our Heavenly Father! I do not care how disturbing your life seems; you keep pushing, believing things are working out. God does the impossible, so we cannot ever take full credit and think we are functioning on our own. He wants to get all the glory—not for you, but for someone else who may be going through something in life.

Don't ever give up on your dreams. Remember, setbacks are preparing you for your purpose in life. You came here to serve a specific plan, and everything that's happened thus far was designed for your mission. Live fearlessly, and don't apologize for who you are becoming. Don't let excuses be your crutch for why things are not happening. Don't go ahead of God or try to force anything. Learn how to listen to the soft whisper, it is your GPS for your world.

Life will throw some unexpected scenarios at you, but as long you know you can do all things through Christ who strengthens you, you will get past the hurdle. Life will have its ups and downs, but they're all part of your trip. It is how you tackle the downtime that will determine the result of the next chapter. I do not even understand why people get so depressed when things are not going their way; this is your consciousness trying to teach you valuable lessons. These very moments usually push you toward being who you were created to be.

It is easy to be happy when things are going our way. What's hard about that? However, the challenge comes when push comes to shove. Are you able to keep the joy? Oh, trust me, you can talk the talk when everything you want is manifesting. But can you walk the walk when everything seems to be falling apart, when every door seems to be shutting on you and nothing is making sense?

Queen, raise your chin up, straighten your crown, and keep pushing. You are royal because your father is King of the entire universe. You are going to come out of this vigorous and exceptional.

Life is full of surprises and miracles. You do not know what God has in store for you. Learn how to accept each day the way it unfolds. The Lord is the only one who knows what the next step is. This book has been written moment by moment for the past two years. It will show you that life is not black and white. There are many twists and turns on every page, but when you know your purpose and have a firm belief in God with unwavering faith, God will unfold it perfectly. I hope that you do not look at dark seasons as bad moments, but as character-building moments. You are developing mental toughness as long as you do not allow them to break you.

I share this to hopefully enlighten you about life. Everyone is always going through something. I recently heard, "In life you are either going into a storm, going through a storm, or coming out of a storm." In a nutshell, we will always have painful moments, but all of them are being used to bring you closer to your calling. If you can modify your mindset and look at obstacle seasons as possibilities, this will refine your whole way of thinking, especially when you are going through a hardship.

God will give you peace and people will not even understand how you can be so calm about the predicament you are facing. However, I can promise it will make people curious, and you can touch people's lives by being an example how it looks to trust and have faith in our Heavenly Father. Are you walking the talk or are you just talking? Be the person God can trust with whatever life fires at them. Be the person who can look at life's problems and wink at them. Remember, your perception is your reality. Change your thoughts and your world around you will change. Our Heavenly Father cares about our well-being. He wants to see us doing amazing things in life. Count your blessings instead of looking at the things that are not going your way.

Many times when I start thinking about what's going wrong, I pause and reflect on how many great things are currently going on. You can always find the good things happening in your life. Humans can naturally gravitate to the negative, but we need to rewire our brains and control our thoughts. When I started to change my thoughts, things started changing for me. Just remember, this, too, shall pass. Thank your ex for walking away. Miracles are constantly unfolding in front of you, but it's going to take a pure heart and mind to recognize them. It's going to take you being still, listening to God, and reading His word. Rewrite your story. What do you want the next chapter of your life to say?

Love you and take care,

Angelina Rosario

ABOUT THE AUTHOR

Angelina Rosario is a sales leader, coach, author, entrepreneur, and overcomer. She has influenced thousands of women by teaching them that trials and setbacks are their secret weapons in achieving success and becoming their best version of themselves.

Born and raised in Miami, Angelina inspires others to live and dream big. She and her two sisters were raised in the projects in Miami by their single mother. Angelina worked hard to change the trajectory of her life and went from being a statistic to a success story.

In the years following a major breakup, Angelina attended relationship workshops, hired a relationship coach, read all the books on how to get over a heartbreak, and discovered that heartbreak could instead be an uncompromising teacher of authenticity, power, purpose, and even joy.

In 2017, Angelina launched She Fixes Crowns, a company to teach women how to go from mediocre to excellent in every area of their lives. Her vision is to empower women to leave a legacy for generations to come. She teaches women by using her own experiences and methods she applied to become a boss babe.

Angelina also underwent four major surgeries in four years due to a tumor the size of a baseball in her face. While in intensive care and being fed through a tube, she made a promise to God that if He would get her through her surgeries, she would devote her life to helping women. She didn't allow obstacles to make her lose sight of her purpose. Even though the odds were stacked against her, she was determined not to allow conditions to stop her from achieving her goals and using her pain toward purpose.

Because Angelina has a heart for women, on any given day, you can find her pouring into the lives of other women by speaking positive words and sowing seeds to assist on how to heal from a broken heart, promote healthy lifestyles, or how to be successful in the business world. Because of her faith, obedience, hard work, and dedication, she was able to turn her storms into blessings. She achieved her success by walking the talk. Instead of focusing on fear, pain, and difficult days, she decided to endure and focus on the promise.

When Angelina is not leading the sales department in the media industry, giving seminars, writing, or speaking, she enjoys working out, reading, traveling, and spending time with her family and friends.